T0285131

ALSO AVAILABLE IN THIS SERIES

Year A, Volume 2

Season after Pentecost

 Connections

Worship Companion

David Gambrell, editor

WESTMINSTER
JOHN KNOX PRESS
LOUISVILLE • KENTUCKY

© 2023 Westminster John Knox Press

First Edition
Published by Westminster John Knox Press
Louisville, Kentucky

24 25 26 27 28 29 30 31 32 — 10 9 8 7 6 5 4 3 2

Book design by Drew Stevens
Cover design by Allison Taylor

Library of Congress Cataloging-in-Publication Data

Names: Gambrell, David, editor.
Title: Connections worship companion : Year C / David Gambrell.
Description: First edition. | Louisville, Kentucky : Westminster John Knox
    Press, 2021. | Series: Connections: a lectionary commentary for
    preaching and worship | Includes index. | Summary: "Part of the
    Connections commentary series, these worship resources help
    congregations illuminate the connections between Scripture and
    liturgical rhythms. A "Making Connections" essay precedes each
    liturgical season's resources, providing context for worship within the
    themes and purpose of the season"-- Provided by publisher.
Identifiers: LCCN 2021023009 (print) | LCCN 2021023010 (ebook) | ISBN
    9780664264963 (hardback) | ISBN 9781646982080 (ebook)
Subjects: LCSH: Common lectionary (1992). Year C. | Public worship. |
    Worship programs.
Classification: LCC BV199.L42 C66 2021 (print) | LCC BV199.L42 (ebook) |
    DDC 264.05--dc23
LC record available at https://lccn.loc.gov/2021023009
LC ebook record available at https://lccn.loc.gov/2021023010

Connections Worship Companion, Year A, Volume 2
ISBN: 9780664264932 (hardback)
ISBN: 9781646983155 (ebook)

Contents

Supplements for the Narrative Lectionary

Introduction

This is not a book of prayers—
at least not yet.

These words will not become prayers
until the Holy Spirit breathes them,
until the body of Christ speaks and hears them,
until the people of God live them
in acts of service and love.

These words come from different people
in different places of ministry—
pastors and poets,
students and scholars,
activists and artists,
evangelists and educators,
bakers and baristas,
mission workers and musicians.

They have different voices,
and those voices will resonate
with different worshipers
in different ways.

It will be up to you,
as a planner and leader of worship,
to make these words sing:

to pray them
among the beloved people of God
with honesty, passion, wonder, and grace;

to enact them
as the whole body of Christ
with heart, mind, soul, and strength;

to transform them
through the gifts of the Spirit,
with rhythm, color, texture, and taste.

You are encouraged, then,
even challenged,
even required
to find your own voice,
to inhabit these texts,
to adapt them as needed,
so that these words
may become the prayers
of your people
in your place
for the sake of the world,
all people,
in every place.

Only then
will these words become prayers.

Only then
will they rise like incense before God,
joining the intercession
of our great high priest,
Christ Jesus,
who still teaches us to pray.

David Gambrell

How to Use This Book

Three kinds of materials are provided in this volume. First, at the beginning of each major section is a short essay titled "Making Connections." These brief passages of commentary have several purposes:

- they introduce the primary theological themes of a given time in the Christian year;
- they highlight a particular biblical text, drawn from the lectionary, that may be used as a kind of lens for magnifying and examining the themes of the season;
- they point to distinctive features of the lectionary cycle included in this volume; and

- they offer practical and pastoral guidance for leaders as they seek to prepare faithful, thoughtful, creative, and engaging worship for the people of God.

These essays can be used in discussion with worship committees, planning teams, or church staff groups to promote biblical study, inspire theological reflection, and inform liturgical action.

Second, each section includes a collection of seasonal/repeating resources. These are liturgical texts intended for use during a certain span of time in the Christian year, whether occasionally or for several weeks in a row. Specifically, these resources include the following acts of worship:

Confession and Pardon
Prayer for Illumination
Thanksgiving for Baptism
Great Thanksgiving
Prayer after Communion
Prayer of Thanksgiving (for the dedication of the offering when the Eucharist is not celebrated)
Blessing

These texts are somewhat broader and more general in their theological content and liturgical language, and they are designed for multiple uses within a liturgical season or period of Ordinary Time. They promote diachronic (meaning "through time") connections from one Sunday to the next, deriving their benefit from regular engagement with the church's tradition as people return to worship from week to week. They emphasize central convictions of Christian faith and life, supporting the kind of faith formation that takes place through sustained, long-term participation in worship. These texts are especially connected with the celebration of the sacraments.

Third, there is a set of resources for each Sunday or festival in the Christian year. Specifically, these resources include the following elements of the service:

Opening Sentences (or Call to Worship)
Prayer of the Day (or Gathering Prayer)
Invitation to Discipleship
Prayers of Intercession
Invitation to Offering
Invitation to the Table
Charge

These texts are somewhat narrower and more specific in their theological content and liturgical language, and they are designed for use on a given Sunday or festival in the Christian year. They promote synchronic (meaning "same time") connections between the liturgy and the lectionary, deriving their benefit from flashes of insight that collect around a common word, image, or phrase from the biblical texts for the day. They emphasize particular practices of Christian faith and life, supporting the kind of faith formation that takes place in more concentrated, short-term experiences of worship. These texts are especially connected with the proclamation of the word.

By combining the **seasonal/repeating resources (in bold type)** with the *Sunday/festival elements (in italics)*, as well as other elements not provided in this resource (in regular type), as indicated below, worship planners will be able to assemble complete orders of worship for the Lord's Day.

GATHERING

> *Opening Sentences*
> Hymn, Psalm, or Spiritual Song
> *Prayer of the Day*
> **Confession and Pardon**

WORD

> **Prayer for Illumination**
> Scripture
> Sermon
> Hymn, Psalm, or Spiritual Song
> Affirmation of Faith
> *Invitation to Discipleship*
> **Thanksgiving for Baptism**
> *Prayers of Intercession*

EUCHARIST

> *Invitation to Offering*
> Offering
> *Invitation to the Table*
> **Great Thanksgiving**
> Communion
> **Prayer after Communion**

[IF THE EUCHARIST IS OMITTED]

> *Invitation to Offering*
> Offering
>
> **Prayer of Thanksgiving**

SENDING

> Hymn, Psalm, or Spiritual Song
> **Blessing** and *Charge*

This order of worship is offered as one example. The actions and elements of worship may of course be arranged in a variety of other ways according to denominational patterns and congregational practices. This resource is also available in ebook format, from which users can copy and paste liturgies for use in bulletins and other worship materials.

Lectionary Readings

This resource is designed to support and equip users of the three-year Revised Common Lectionary (1992), developed by the ecumenical Consultation on Common Texts as an adaptation and expansion of the Common Lectionary (1983). The contents and composition of this volume reflect that emphasis, consistent with the Connections commentary series.

However, this resource also includes supplemental liturgical materials for the four-year Narrative Lectionary (2010), designed by faculty at Luther Seminary in St. Paul, Minnesota. Taking advantage of overlap between the two systems, with these supplemental materials, this resource will address (at least obliquely) all of the primary texts of the Narrative Lectionary over the course of its six volumes.

See the Scripture index for the list of the lectionary readings supported in this volume (in canonical order). A comprehensive index of Years A, B, and C is available at www.wjkbooks.com/CONindex.

Acknowledgments

Contributors to this volume include Claudia L. Aguilar Rubalcava, Mamie Broadhurst, Marci Auld Glass, Marcus A. Hong, Kimberly Bracken Long, Emily McGinley, Kendra L. Buckwalter Smith, Samuel Son, Slats Toole, and Byron A. Wade. Their deep faith, pastoral wisdom, creative gifts, and fervent prayers are the lifeblood of this work. The editor also expresses deep gratitude to David Maxwell, vice president for curriculum and church resources at Westminster John Knox Press, for his guidance in the development of this project, and to Jessica Miller Kelley, senior acquisitions editor at Westminster John Knox Press, for shepherding it to completion.

Key to Symbols and Abbreviations

Regular	Leader
Bold	People
Italics	Rubric describing liturgical action or identifying options
. . .	Time for individual prayers, spoken or silent
or	Alternate readings or responses

Resources for the Revised Common Lectionary

SEASON AFTER PENTECOST

Making Connections

In the time after Pentecost, Year A of the Revised Common Lectionary follows the life, teaching, and ministry of Jesus according to the Gospel of Matthew. The lectionary sets the stage for this journey on Trinity Sunday with the Great Commission, Jesus' final words in Matthew: "Go therefore and make disciples of all nations" (Matt. 28:19). Then through the rest of Year A, it presents the example of Jesus' own travels from Galilee to Jerusalem, making disciples and teaching them the ways of the realm of God. Depending on the date of Easter (and the subsequent dates of Pentecost and Trinity Sunday), we join the Gospel narrative at some point between Jesus' Sermon on the Mount (Matt. 5:1–7:29) and his instructions for the mission of the Twelve (Matt. 9:35–11:1). Significant and distinctive passages include the parable of the house built on rock (Matt. 7:21–29), an invitation to take up the yoke of Christ (Matt. 11:16–19, 25–30), stories about seeds and soil (Matt. 13:1–9, 18–23), the pearl of great price (Matt. 13:31–33, 44–52), Jesus and Peter walking on the water (Matt. 14:22–33), the call to forgive seventy-seven times (Matt. 18:21–35), laborers in a vineyard (Matt. 20:1–16), and a lesson about the coin used for taxes (Matt. 22:15–22). Worship planners might find creative ways to use these visual symbols in the time after Pentecost. In the final weeks of the Christian year, the lectionary readings anticipate Advent by highlighting eschatological concerns: a call for vigilance (Matt. 25:1–13), a parable about faithful stewardship (Matt. 25:14–30), and an account of final judgment (Matt. 25:31–46). This presents an opportunity to preach and pray about the nature of Christian hope as we watch for Christ's coming again in glory.

There are two tracks of readings from the Old Testament in the time after Pentecost: the *semicontinuous* readings, which move in sequence through major stories and themes of the Hebrew Scriptures, and the *complementary* readings, which are connected with the events and images of the Gospel readings. The semicontinuous readings in Year A focus on the earliest accounts of the people of God, from the five books of the *Torah* (Genesis through Deuteronomy) through the entry into the land of Canaan (Joshua and Judges). Roughly half of these readings (thirteen weeks) feature the ancestral narratives of Genesis, including the stories of Abraham and Sarah; Isaac and

Rebekah; Jacob, Esau, Leah, and Rachel; and Joseph and his siblings. Prominent themes include promise, providence, faith, sacrifice, betrayal, sibling rivalry, liberation, law, and covenant. In this time after Pentecost, worship planners might find imaginative ways to review the "family album" of our forebears in the faith. The complementary readings in Year A, selected in coordination with the Gospel readings, come from a great array of Old Testament books: Genesis, Exodus, Leviticus, Deuteronomy, 1 Kings, Isaiah, Jeremiah, Ezekiel, Hosea, Jonah, Micah, Zephaniah, and Zechariah. These intertextual connections demonstrate how the whole canon of Scripture bears witness to Jesus as God's Word made flesh.

In the design of the Revised Common Lectionary, psalms and canticles (other biblical songs) are intended to be musical and prayerful responses to the first reading (typically Hebrew Scripture, or Acts during the season of Easter). Preachers will find strong connections between the first reading and the psalm or canticle; however, remember that the psalms and canticles are specific to their Old Testament track (semicontinuous or complementary) and thus not interchangeable. Worship planners might use the lectionary psalms and canticles in guiding the choice of hymns for the day, drawing on metrical settings of the psalms, for example.

The second readings present a series of sequential selections from New Testament epistles, featuring Romans (sixteen weeks), Philippians (four weeks), and 1 Thessalonians (five weeks). The extended use of Paul's letter to the church at Rome offers leaders a chance to highlight the important theological themes of sin and salvation, justification by grace through faith, the nature of Christian hope, the relationship between Israel and the church, and the transforming work of God in the lives of believers. Worship planners might be attentive for ways to accent these topics in the second half of the Christian year.

At the beginning of the time after Pentecost, on Trinity Sunday of Year A, we hear the promise of Jesus: "I am with you always, to the end of the age" (Matt. 28:20). On the Reign of Christ Sunday, as we come to the conclusion of Year A and the time after Pentecost, Jesus reveals that he has indeed been with us all along, but in a surprising way—whenever we care for those who are hungry and thirsty, strangers or naked, sick or in prison. "Truly I tell you," Jesus says, "just as you did it to one of the least of these who are members of my family, you did it to me" (Matt. 25:40). Through our year with Matthew we have come to know, trust, and worship the living God who dwells among us in humble human form—the one we call Emmanuel, "God with us" (Matt. 1:23).

Seasonal/Repeating Resources

These resources are intended for regular use throughout the time after Pentecost.

CONFESSION AND PARDON

1 Based on Genesis; especially appropriate for Trinity Sunday through Proper 15

The confession and pardon may be led from the baptismal font.

> We are dust,
> and to dust we shall return.
> Yet into this dust
> God has breathed the Spirit of life.
> Into this dust
> God pours out the gift of grace.
>
> Trusting in God's grace, let us confess our sin.

The confession may begin with a time of silence for personal prayer.

> **God of our ancestors,**
> **you have remained faithful to us**
> **from generation to generation.**
> **But we have broken our promises.**
> **We hear your plans for us**
> **and we laugh in disbelief.**
> **We test your patience**
> **and question your providence.**
> **We bargain away our birthright**
> **and grasp at what is not ours.**
> **We succumb to jealous rivalry**
> **and betray those we love.**

Forgive us, we pray.
Recreate us as your people,
and restore us to your image.
Continue to bless us,
and let us be a blessing for others.
Keep us in your mercy,
and cover us with your grace;
through Jesus Christ our Lord.

Water may be poured or lifted from the baptismal font.

God has made an everlasting covenant with us:
to preserve us from destruction, despite our sin.
When the clouds come and the rain falls
we see the rainbow and remember God's promise—
the gift of overflowing mercy and abundant grace.

In the name of Jesus Christ, we are forgiven.
Thanks be to God.

2 Based on Matthew 18; especially appropriate for Propers 18–19

The confession and pardon may be led from the baptismal font.

Jesus calls us,
as members of the church,
to be accountable to God and to one another:
confessing our sin,
repairing the damage done,
and working together for reconciliation.
And Jesus promises
that he will be with us in this work,
whenever two or three gather in his name.

Trusting in God's grace, let us confess our sin.

The confession may begin with a time of silence for personal prayer.

Gracious God, in Jesus Christ
you have taught us to pray,
"Forgive us our debts
as we forgive our debtors."

Yet even as we depend on your mercy,
we fail to extend such mercy to others.
We hold onto old grudges,
count up the sins of others,
and seek to settle the score.

Gracious God, forgive us,
and open our hearts to forgive one another.
Pour out your grace upon us,
and let it overflow into the lives of others.
Let your church be a living sign
of your reconciling love for all the world;
through Jesus Christ our Lord.

Water may be poured or lifted from the baptismal font.

We are forgiven,
we are forgiven,
we are forgiven—
for the things we have done
and the things we have failed to do.

We are forgiven,
we are forgiven,
we are forgiven—
for our sins against God
and our sins against one another.

We are forgiven—
not just seven times,
or seventy-seven times,
or even seventy times seven,
but over and over and always.

In the name of Jesus Christ, we are forgiven.
Thanks be to God.

3 Based on Romans; especially appropriate for Propers 4–19

The confession and pardon may be led from the baptismal font.

> All have sinned and fall short of the glory of God.
> But we are justified by God's grace as a gift,
> through the redemption that is ours in Christ Jesus.
>
> Trusting in God's grace, let us confess our sin.

The confession may begin with a time of silence for personal prayer.

> **Loving God,**
> **while we were sinners**
> **you sent Christ to die for us**
> **that we might be justified**
> **by grace through faith**
> **and have peace with you.**
> **Yet we continue to live in sin.**
> **We know what is good and right,**
> **but we do what is hateful and evil.**
> **We live according to the flesh**
> **and resist the work of the Spirit.**
> **We reject and deny your calling**
> **to the other children of Abraham.**
> **We fail to love our neighbors**
> **and thereby fail to fulfill your law.**
> **We do not contribute to those in need**
> **or extend hospitality to strangers.**
> **We ignore the groaning of creation**
> **and forget the hope of the gospel.**
>
> **Forgive us, loving God.**
> **Pour out your Spirit into our hearts,**
> **that we may learn to live as those**
> **who are dead to sin and alive to you;**
> **through Jesus Christ our Lord.**

Water may be poured or lifted from the baptismal font.

What can separate us from the love of Christ?
Nothing.
Neither death, nor life,
nor heavenly beings, nor earthly powers,
nor things present, nor things to come,
nor height, nor depth,
nor anything else in all creation
will be able to separate us
from the love of God
in Christ Jesus our Lord.

In the name of Jesus Christ, we are forgiven.
Thanks be to God.

PRAYER FOR ILLUMINATION

1 **Based on Genesis 1; especially appropriate for Trinity Sunday**

The prayer for illumination is led from the lectern or pulpit.

God of light,
whose Spirit shaped the sun
and scattered the stars,
shine your light upon your Word,
that we may see your truth
and follow your way;
for the sake of Jesus Christ,
the light of the world. **Amen.**

2 **Based on Exodus 19–20 and Psalm 19; especially appropriate for Proper 6, complementary, and Proper 22, semicontinuous**

The prayer for illumination is led from the lectern or pulpit.

Holy God,
you have given us your law
that we might have abundant life.
By your Spirit,
open our ears to your Word
and our hearts to your will,
that we may live in your light
and live out your love;
for the sake of Jesus Christ our Savior. **Amen.**

3 Based on Romans 10:5–15; especially appropriate for Proper 14

The prayer for illumination is led from the lectern or pulpit.

> Holy God, draw near to us,
> and by the gift of your Spirit
> let the word of our faith
> be on our lips and in our hearts.
> Send us forth to proclaim good news,
> that others may hear and believe,
> calling on the saving name
> of Jesus Christ our Lord. **Amen.**

THANKSGIVING FOR BAPTISM

1 Based on Exodus 14–15; especially appropriate for Proper 19

The thanksgiving for baptism is led from the baptismal font.

The introductory dialogue ("The Lord be with you . . .") may be sung or spoken.

> Saving God,
> you deliver us from slavery to freedom.
> **All thanks and praise to you, O God!**
>
> You guide us through the darkness of night
> and bring us to safety with the morning light.
> **All thanks and praise to you, O God!**
>
> You part the waters of the sea,
> sparing us from chaos and death;
> in the face of evil,
> you make a way where there is no way.
> **All thanks and praise to you, O God!**
>
> Gracious God,
> you are our salvation,
> our strength, and our song.
> You quench our thirst with sweet, sweet water,
> pouring out your unending love.

You claim us as your own
in the waters of baptism,
that we might know we belong to you.

For the water of life, we give you thanks
and rejoice that we are baptized:
**All thanks and praise to you, O God,
now and forever! Amen.**

2 Based on Romans 6:1b–11; especially appropriate for Proper 7

The thanksgiving for baptism is led from the baptismal font.

The introductory dialogue ("The Lord be with you . . .") may be sung or spoken.

Holy God,
in the waters of baptism you save us from death
and deliver us to everlasting life with Christ.
You free us from the grip of sin
and give us power to walk in newness of life.

By your Spirit
you raise us up
and set us free.
You pour out grace upon grace,
making us one with our Savior and Lord.

We thank you, most gracious God,
for living our life
and dying our death,
that we might live eternally with you.
May our lips continually sing your praise
and our lives be thank offerings to you,
for the sake of Jesus Christ, our Redeemer. **Amen.**

3 Based on Philippians 2:1–13; especially appropriate for Proper 21

The thanksgiving for baptism is led from the baptismal font.

The introductory dialogue ("The Lord be with you . . .") may be sung or spoken.

Holy One, we give you thanks and praise
for the baptism we share with Christ Jesus—
who did not take advantage of his divinity,
but emptied himself, taking human form,
and gave up his life on the cross.
Great is the mystery of faith:
Christ has died.

Holy One, we give you thanks and praise
for the resurrection we share with Christ Jesus—
who is risen from the dead and highly exalted,
and to whom you have given the name
that is above every name in heaven and earth.
Great is the mystery of faith:
Christ is risen.

Holy One, we give you thanks and praise
for the eternal hope we share with Christ Jesus—
who is coming again in glory to reign
on the day when every knee will bend
and every tongue confess him Lord.
Great is the mystery of faith:
Christ will come again.

Glory to you, holy triune God,
Spirit, Savior, and Sovereign,
now and forever. **Amen.**

GREAT THANKSGIVING

1 Based on the Pentateuch, the books of Genesis through Deuteronomy; appropriate throughout the time after Pentecost

The Great Thanksgiving is led from the Communion table.

The introductory dialogue ("The Lord be with you . . .") may be sung or spoken.

>Blessed are you, O God,
>Maker of heaven and earth.
>In the beginning, you spoke—
>calling all things into being,
>claiming a covenant people,
>choosing them to be a blessing.
>You are the source of life;
>you are the land of promise;
>you are the hope of generations.
>
>For your love and faithfulness
>we give you thanks and praise,
>joining the hymns of our ancestors:

The Sanctus ("Holy, holy, holy . . .") may be sung or spoken.

>Blessed are you, O God,
>Savior and Sovereign of all.
>Out of captivity, you called us—
>redeeming us from oppression,
>leading us through the waters,
>delivering us from death to life.
>You are the bread of heaven;
>you are living water from a stone;
>you are the Lord, the great I AM.

The words of institution are included here, if not elsewhere, while the bread and cup are lifted (but not broken/poured).

>As we receive this holy meal
>we remember Christ our passover,
>proclaiming the mystery of faith:

A memorial acclamation ("Christ has died . . .") may be sung or spoken.

Blessed are you, O God,
Spirit of wisdom and joy.
In this assembly, you pour out grace—
transforming the bread and the cup,
revealing the flesh and the blood,
building up the body of Christ.
You are our daily destination;
you are our earthly pilgrimage;
you are our heavenly home.

With heart and soul and might
we will love and serve you alone,
glorifying your holy name. **Amen.**

A Trinitarian doxology and Great Amen may be sung or spoken.

2 Based on Matthew; appropriate throughout Year A

The Great Thanksgiving is led from the Communion table.

The introductory dialogue ("The Lord be with you . . .") may be sung or spoken.

God of heaven and earth,
you spoke the world into being
and called it good.
Thank you for the mystery and beauty of the cosmos,
for the wonder of this planet on which you have placed us,
for breathing life into us and all you have created.
Thank you for making a covenant with us,
for guiding our feet by your law
and turning us around through your prophets.

The Sanctus ("Holy, holy, holy . . .") may be sung or spoken.

Thank you especially for the gift of your Son,
the fulfillment of your law and prophets.
He lived and breathed as one of us,
teaching us the ways of blessing
and showing us the kingdom of heaven.

He fed us, healed us,
and commissioned us
to be salt of the earth and light of the world.
He even died with us and for us,
that we might live with you for all eternity
in your just and peaceful realm.

Thank you for the gift of this meal he shares with us,
a foretaste of your heavenly banquet.

We thank you that Jesus, on the night he was arrested,
took bread and blessed it and broke it
to give to his disciples,
his own body given for them, and for us.

We thank you that he shared the cup,
the new covenant sealed in his blood,
shed for us for the forgiveness of sins.
Whenever we share this meal,
we do it in remembrance of him.

A memorial acclamation ("Christ has died . . .") may be sung or spoken.

Thank you, too,
for your Holy Spirit,
our Advocate.
By your Spirit
we offer ourselves to you
as a sacrifice of praise.
Through your Spirit
may these gifts of bread and wine
be Christ's body and blood for us.

Feed us once again, O God.
Make us one, make us whole,
that we may indeed be salt and light
for the world you so love.
All thanks and praise to you, triune God,
now and forever. **Amen.**

A Trinitarian doxology and Great Amen may be sung or spoken.

3 Based on Romans; especially appropriate for Propers 4–19

The Great Thanksgiving is led from the Communion table.

The introductory dialogue ("The Lord be with you . . .") may be sung or spoken.

> God of grace,
> **we give you thanks and praise.**
>
> Your Word formed creation,
> your breath gave us life,
> your law taught us how to live.
> When we could not follow your ways,
> your prophets called us back to you.
> And when the time was right,
> you sent your only Son
> to die a death like ours,
> so that we might live a life like his,
> eternally with you.
> God of grace,
> **we give you thanks and praise.**

The Sanctus ("Holy, holy, holy . . .") may be sung or spoken.

> While he walked with us,
> Jesus fed us:
> by his words,
> with his hands,
> through his love.
> Before he died,
> he shared a meal with his disciples,
> blessing the bread that was his body,
> sharing the cup that was his blood,
> urging us to remember
> the life he lived,
> showing us how to anticipate
> your realm that is to come.
> God of grace,
> **we give you thanks and praise.**

The words of institution are included here, if not elsewhere, while the bread and cup are lifted (but not broken/poured).

A memorial acclamation ("Christ has died . . .") may be sung or spoken.

> By your Spirit, O God,
> make this bread and wine
> the body and blood of Christ for us.
> Feed our aching hearts,
> renew our hope in future glory,
> and send us out to proclaim your love,
> the love from which no thing,
> and no one,
> can separate us.
> God of grace,
> **we give you thanks and praise.**

> All thanks and praise to you, O God,
> Creator, Redeemer, Sustainer,
> Father, Son, and Holy Spirit,
> One God, now and forever. **Amen.**

A Trinitarian doxology and Great Amen may be sung or spoken.

PRAYER AFTER COMMUNION

1 Based on Exodus 16:2–15; especially appropriate for Proper 20

The prayer after Communion is led from the Communion table.

> O Lord our God, we give you thanks
> for the bread of heaven we have shared,
> a generous gift of your abundant grace.
> Teach us to share our daily bread,
> that all may have enough for each day
> and enjoy the fullness of life you offer;
> through Jesus Christ our Savior. **Amen.**

2 Based on Matthew 25:31–46; especially appropriate for the Reign of Christ Sunday

The prayer after Communion is led from the Communion table.

> Thanks be to you, Lord Jesus Christ.
> We came to you hungry and thirsty;
> you nourished us with your body
> and shared the cup of salvation.
> We came to you strangers and naked;
> you welcomed us as beloved ones
> and clothed us with your grace.
> We came to you sick and imprisoned;
> you delivered us from death
> and set us free from our sin.
> Now send us forth from this table
> to seek you in the faces of our neighbors
> and to give as we have received—
> feeding others and giving them drink,
> welcoming strangers and clothing the naked,
> healing the sick and setting captives free—
> that we may all find a place together
> at the heavenly banquet you prepare.
> In your holy name we pray. **Amen.**

3 Based on Revelation 7:9–17; especially appropriate for All Saints' Day

The prayer after Communion is led from the Communion table.

> God of earth and heaven,
> thank you for meeting us at this table,
> for feeding us, healing us, and giving us strength.
> Thank you for a taste of the joy that is to come—
> when every tear will be wiped away,
> when no one will hunger or thirst,
> and when we will drink from the springs of the water of life.
> Blessing and glory and wisdom
> and thanksgiving and honor
> and power and might be to you, O God,
> forever and ever! **Amen.**

PRAYER OF THANKSGIVING

1 Based on Matthew 22:15–22; especially appropriate for Proper 24

The prayer of thanksgiving may be led from the Communion table.

> Holy God,
> Maker of heaven and earth,
> all things come from you
> and to you all things belong.
> We thank you for making us in your image
> and claiming us as your beloved people.
> With gratitude for your grace,
> we dedicate these gifts to you.
> Use them in the service of your eternal realm
> and for the sake of the mission
> of Jesus Christ our Lord. **Amen.**

2 Based on Romans 12; especially appropriate for Propers 16–17

The prayer of thanksgiving may be led from the Communion table.

> Merciful God, we give you thanks
> that you have given us many different gifts
> for service in the one body of Christ.
> We present ourselves to you
> as a living sacrifice of praise.
> Use us—our gifts and offerings—
> to do your will in the world:
> contributing to those in need,
> making peace with our neighbors,
> and overcoming evil with good;
> through Jesus Christ our Savior. **Amen.**

3 Based on Philippians 2–3; especially appropriate for Propers 21–22

The prayer of thanksgiving may be led from the Communion table.

> Gracious God, we give you thanks
> for the self-giving love of Jesus Christ,
> who emptied himself for us
> that we might have fullness of life in him.
> Receive the offering of our lives.
> Use these humble, human gifts
> to bring glory to your holy name.
> Teach us the surpassing value
> of knowing Jesus Christ as Lord.
> And keep us pressing forward in faith
> until we share the heavenly calling
> of our crucified and risen Savior. **Amen.**

BLESSING

1 Based on Matthew 28:16–20; especially appropriate for Trinity Sunday or throughout Year A

The blessing and charge may be led from the doors of the church.

> The blessing of God the Father,
> God the Son,
> and God the Holy Spirit
> be with you, now and always,
> to the end of the age. **Alleluia!**

2 Based on 2 Corinthians 13:11–13; especially appropriate for Trinity Sunday

The blessing and charge may be led from the doors of the church.

> The grace of the Lord Jesus Christ
> be with you. **Alleluia!**
>
> The love of God
> be with you. **Alleluia!**
>
> The communion of the Holy Spirit
> be with you. **Alleluia!**

3 Based on Philippians 4:1–9; especially appropriate for Propers 20–23

The blessing and charge may be led from the doors of the church.

> The peace of God be with you,
> surpassing all understanding.
> The peace of Christ be with you,
> guarding your hearts and minds.
> The peace of the Spirit be with you,
> filling you with joy. **Alleluia!**

Trinity Sunday

Genesis 1:1–2:4a   2 Corinthians 13:11–13
Psalm 8   Matthew 28:16–20

OPENING SENTENCES

> O Lord, our Lord,
> how majestic is your name in all the earth!
> **When I consider your heavens,**
> **the work of your fingers,**
> **the moon and the stars**
> **you have set in their courses,**
>
> what are mere mortals
> that you should be mindful of them,
> human beings that you should care for them?
> **Yet you have made them little less than divine;**
> **with glory and honor you crown them.**
>
> You have given them dominion over the works of your hands;
> you have put all things under their feet:
> all flocks and cattle, the beasts of the field,
> the birds of the air, the fish of the sea.
> **O Lord, our Lord,**
> **how majestic is your name in all the earth!**

PRAYER OF THE DAY

> Holy God, Three-in-One,
> from the communion of your being,
> love overflowed,
> endowing us with your image
> and calling us into community.
> Help us to listen for your word,
> that our lives may be ordered
> by your peace alone;
> through Jesus Christ our Lord. **Amen.**

INVITATION TO DISCIPLESHIP

The invitation to discipleship may be led from the baptismal font.

The God who set the stars in the heavens
cares profoundly for you.
The Spirit who brought order out of chaos
longs to fill you with peace.
The Living Word who spoke creation into being
offers purpose for your life.

So come!
In the name of the triune God,
you are welcome here
among this community of disciples.

PRAYERS OF INTERCESSION

The prayers of intercession may be led from the midst of the congregation.

God of mystery, in your triune being,
you show us what it is to be community—
creating space for others,
working in concert and peace,
discovering unity in love.
You invite us, as your people,
to gather the world's needs into our hearts
and bring them before you in prayer.

Heavenly Parent, loving Creator,
from depth of sea to soaring sky,
each intricate detail of creation
bears witness to your mindful care.
Where thoughtlessness poisons the waters and pollutes the air,
where greed ravishes the earth
and disturbs the rhythm of your creatures,
call us once again to be stewards of your creation.

Eternal Son, blessed Savior,
from lowly estate to halls of power,
the promise of your presence
leads us to your grace and peace.
Where self-protection creates barriers and threatens war,
where intolerance separates one from another,
call us once again to make disciples of all nations.

Enlivening Spirit, constant Companion,
from hidden corners of our hearts
to the communion of saints,
the winds of creative imagination
nudge us to your power and wisdom.
Where the grip of doubt, depression, or despair lays claim,
where inhumanity perpetuates oppression,
call us once again to live in your abiding presence.

Triune God,
within us, between us,
among us, embracing us,
receive the prayers of our hearts
for the sake of your beloved creation.
Through Christ who lives and reigns with you
in the communion of the Holy Spirit,
one God now and forever. **Amen.**

INVITATION TO OFFERING

The invitation to offering may be led from the Communion table.

God's call to us
is woven into the very fabric of creation.
For God has given to us every good thing,
entrusting us to be stewards of all we have received.

Made in the image of the triune God,
let us share God's grace and love and fellowship
through the offering of our gifts.

INVITATION TO THE TABLE

The invitation to the table is led from the Communion table.

By the mysterious wonder of our triune God,
we are gathered in this time to celebrate a feast for all time.

In the beginning,
God caused grains to spring forth from the earth
and grapes to grow on the vine—
wheat and wine bringing nourishment and delight.

In the fullness of time,
Christ Jesus gave himself to suffering and death—
body and blood bringing newness of life.

In the end of the age,
the Spirit unites all creation in peace and praise—
light and life bringing eternal communion.

By the mysterious wonder of our triune God,
there is a place for everyone at this table.

CHARGE

The blessing and charge may be led from the doors of the church.

Christ is with you always, to the end of the age.
Go therefore, in the name of the triune God,
and live in peace.
Amen. *or* **Thanks be to God.**

Proper 3

May 24–28, if after Trinity Sunday

Isaiah 49:8–16a   1 Corinthians 4:1–5
Psalm 131   Matthew 6:24–34

OPENING SENTENCES

> When we worry that God
> couldn't possibly know us or care for us,
> God replies through the prophet Isaiah:
> "Can a woman forget her nursing child,
> or show no compassion for the child of her womb?
> Even these may forget, yet I will not forget you.
> See, I have inscribed you on the palms of my hands."

> Let us worship God.

PRAYER OF THE DAY

> Mothering God,
> gather us in your arms and hold us.
> Calm and quiet our souls like a child with its parent.
> Lead us to rest in your embrace,
> that we may be fed and nurtured here this day
> as we worship you with joy and gratitude. **Amen.**

O LORD, my heart is not lifted up, my eyes are not raised too high; I do not occupy myself with things too great and too marvelous for me. But I have calmed and quieted my soul, like a weaned child with its mother.

Psalm 131:1–2a

INVITATION TO DISCIPLESHIP

The invitation to discipleship may be led from the baptismal font.

The apostle Paul calls us
"stewards of God's mysteries."
We aren't called to be explainers, debunkers,
or authors of God's mysteries.
We just get to carry the mystery around,
offering it to others,
so God can reveal whatever needs revealing.

We don't promise easy answers or simple platitudes,
but we invite you to join us
as we seek to steward God's mystery as best we can.
There is room for you here with us
to seek, to serve, and to ponder God's mysteries.

PRAYERS OF INTERCESSION

The prayers of intercession may be led from the midst of the congregation.

O God, who turns mountains into roads
and valleys into flat plains,
we come before you in awe and gratitude.
What are humans that you are mindful of us,
mortals that you care for us?
Thank you for holding us close and for caring for us.
We come before you
confessing that we worry too much,
that we borrow worries from the future.
We offer our worries up to you,
author of our lives and bearer of our burdens.
As we set down those things that weigh us down,
may we be freed to pick up the work
you would have us do.

For your church in every place, hear our prayers.
May we shelter and steward your mysteries,
inviting people to join the journey
and giving safety and shelter to those in need.

For your children in every place, hear our prayers.
May we offer your grace and mercy
to a hurting and anxious world.
May we be agents of your justice and hope,
flattening mountains of racism, classism,
and other forms of injustice,
making a clear path for all.

For your created world, hear our prayers.
May we shelter and protect
the beautiful mystery of your creation,
ensuring a safe world for future generations.

For all whose worries are very real,
and caused by illness, grief, and pain, hear our prayers.
Calm and quiet their souls,
as a parent holds and comforts a child.
Bring your healing, your solace, your wholeness,
so the rough places may be made smooth in their lives.

We offer all these prayers
in the name of your Son, Jesus,
who came that we might have life
and have it abundantly. **Amen.**

INVITATION TO OFFERING

The invitation to offering may be led from the Communion table.

Matthew's Gospel teaches us
to look to the birds of the air
when we're worrying about our lives,
what we will eat, what we will wear.
Jesus teaches us to seek God's kingdom first,
and the rest will follow.

As our offering is received this day,
we give with the confidence of God's beloved children.
Out of our abundance may others find hope.

INVITATION TO THE TABLE

The invitation to the table is led from the Communion table.

The prophet Isaiah writes
that God's people "shall feed along the ways;
on all the bare heights shall be their pasture;
they shall not hunger or thirst,
neither scorching wind nor sun shall strike them down,
for God who has pity on them will lead them
and by springs of water will guide them."

At this table
we come to understand the promise of Isaiah.
Here we find an abundance, like a pasture.
Here we neither hunger nor thirst.
Here we rest in God's shelter and provision.
So come and be fed.
"For the Lord has comforted the people,
and will have compassion on God's suffering ones."

CHARGE

The blessing and charge may be led from the doors of the church.

Jesus calls us to strive first for the kingdom of God
and God's righteousness,
and all these things will be given to us as well.
This week, may you trust in God's provision
as you seek to bring God's realm
to a worried and anxious world.
Go in peace.
Amen. *or* **Thanks be to God.**

Proper 4

May 29–June 4, if after Trinity Sunday

SEMICONTINUOUS READINGS

Genesis 6:9–22; 7:24; 8:14–19   Romans 1:16–17; 3:22b–28 (29–31)
Psalm 46   Matthew 7:21–29

OPENING SENTENCES

God is our refuge and strength,
a very present help in trouble.

The Lord of hosts is with us;
the God of Jacob is our refuge.

PRAYER OF THE DAY

Faithful God,
we know that times of trouble will come.
However, we rest in the assurance
that you will always be with us.
Renew in us your promises
as we gather to worship you.
In the name of your Son
and our Savior, Jesus Christ. **Amen.**

INVITATION TO DISCIPLESHIP

The invitation to discipleship may be led from the baptismal font.

The apostle Paul said,
"I am not ashamed of the gospel;
it is the power of God for salvation."

If you are ready to make a commitment
to follow Christ,
we invite you to become a part
of this community of faith.

PRAYERS OF INTERCESSION

The prayers of intercession may be led from the midst of the congregation.

Let us join our hearts and minds
as we pray together.

O Lord, we lift up our prayers
for places in the world where there is conflict . . .

O Lord, we lift up our prayers
for those who are suffering from illness . . .

O Lord, we pray for those
who are struggling with their faith . . .

O Lord, we pray for those
who feel lost and abandoned . . .

O Lord, we pray for the communities
in which we live . . .

O Lord, we trust that you hear us.
Give us faith that
as we go forth from here,
we will rest in your promises
and seek your will for the world.
We offer these and all our prayers
in the name of your Son, Jesus Christ. **Amen.**

INVITATION TO OFFERING

The invitation to offering may be led from the Communion table.

All that we have is not our own;
it is the Lord's.

Let us return our gifts to the one
who is the gracious giver of all things.

INVITATION TO THE TABLE

The invitation to the table is led from the Communion table.

Hallelujah! The Lord is good
and worthy to be praised.
We know this is true
because God has provided this meal for us
through Jesus Christ.
The invitation to this table
has nothing to do with what we have done;
it is by the grace of God alone.

Come and partake of these gifts!

CHARGE

The blessing and charge may be led from the doors of the church.

Go out into the world with the assurance
that God is always present with us.
Amen. *or* **Thanks be to God.**

Proper 4

May 29–June 4, if after Trinity Sunday

COMPLEMENTARY READINGS

Deuteronomy 11:18–21, 26–28   Romans 1:16–17; 3:22b–28 (29–31)
Psalm 31:1–5, 19–24   Matthew 7:21–29

OPENING SENTENCES

We have come to put your words
into our hearts and souls.
**We have come to teach your words
to our children.**

We are here to remember your promises.
**We are here to remember your love—
to bind it as a sign on our hands
and as an emblem on our foreheads
as we sing, and dance, and pray to you.**

PRAYER OF THE DAY

God of salvation,
incline your ear to us
as we reveal our wounds to you.
Be a rock of refuge
as we crack open our hearts.
Lead us and guide us
as we walk toward the unknown.
We entrust our spirits into your hands. **Amen.**

---

*You shall put these words of mine in your heart and soul, and
you shall bind them as a sign on your hand, and fix them as an
emblem on your forehead. Teach them to your children, talking
about them when you are at home and when you are away, when
you lie down and when you rise.*

Deuteronomy 11:18–19

INVITATION TO DISCIPLESHIP

The invitation to discipleship may be led from the baptismal font.

We have all sinned
and fall short of the glory of God,
yet we have been justified
by God's grace as a gift.

Let us uphold the law of faith
and pour out the love we have received.

PRAYERS OF INTERCESSION

The prayers of intercession may be led from the midst of the congregation.

Ground of our being, today we pray
that we may have the courage
to speak up in the midst of injustice,
as we build our house on bedrock.

We pray for the strength
to dismantle oppressive systems
and level the playing field,
as we build our house on bedrock.

We pray for creativity
to build bridges that may seem impossible,
as we build our house on bedrock.

We pray for a foundation
of compassion and generosity,
as we build our house on bedrock.

We pray for the endurance to resist evil
and the temptation to keep the status quo,
as we build our house on bedrock.

You are the architect of love, O God,
and we are your laborers.
Help us to build our house on bedrock.
All this we pray in the name of Jesus,
the cornerstone of our faith. **Amen.**

INVITATION TO OFFERING

The invitation to offering may be led from the Communion table.

God heard our supplications
when we cried out for help.
What can we give in return?
Our praises and prayers of thanksgiving?
Our time and talents?
Our tithes and offerings?
Our whole lives?

Let us give whatever we can
with a sincere heart.

INVITATION TO THE TABLE

The invitation to the table is led from the Communion table.

Building a house on the rock requires energy.
Our gracious God—
who is architect and farmer,
cook and host—
invites us to pause,
have a moment of rest,
and be fed.

Come to the table.

CHARGE

The blessing and charge may be led from the doors of the church.

Love God, all you saints.
Be strong and let your heart take courage.
God's abundant goodness goes with you.
Amen. *or* **Thanks be to God.**

Proper 5

June 5–11, if after Trinity Sunday

SEMICONTINUOUS READINGS

Genesis 12:1–9

Psalm 33:1–12

Romans 4:13–25

Matthew 9:9–13, 18–26

OPENING SENTENCES

Rejoice in the Lord, O you righteous.
We will praise the Lord!

Sing to the Lord a new song.
We will praise the Lord!

For the Lord has done great things.
We will praise the Lord!

Let us worship God.

PRAYER OF THE DAY

Loving God,
as we enter this place to worship you,
may your Holy Spirit
open our hearts and minds
to experience your presence.
Through our faith journeys,
empower us to bear witness
to your grace, mercy, and power.
In the name of Christ we pray. **Amen.**

---

*For the promise that he would inherit the world did not
come to Abraham or to his descendants through the law
but through the righteousness of faith.*

Romans 4:13

INVITATION TO DISCIPLESHIP

The invitation to discipleship may be led from the baptismal font.

Jesus said to Matthew, "Follow me."

If you are ready to answer Christ's call,
we invite you to follow him.
We are ready to walk with you
in this journey of faith.

PRAYERS OF INTERCESSION

The prayers of intercession may be led from the midst of the congregation.

Merciful God,
we humbly come before you
to pray for ourselves and for one another.
Hear us now as we pray:

for those who are elected leaders . . .

for those who have experienced discrimination
and injustice . . .

for those who have no place to lay their heads . . .

for those who are hurt and broken . . .

for those who face challenges in their faith . . .

for those who have lost loved ones . . .

O God, we know that you love us
and care for each one of your creatures.
Hear our requests and prepare us to witness
the inbreaking of your kin-dom here on earth.
In the name of Jesus Christ we pray. **Amen.**

INVITATION TO OFFERING

The invitation to offering may be led from the Communion table.

The gracious God we serve
has done so much for us!
It is only right
for us to return a portion
of what we have received.

Let us offer our gifts and talents to God.

INVITATION TO THE TABLE

The invitation to the table is led from the Communion table.

Beloved,
you are invited to this table.
It has been set for you
by the goodness and grace
of our Lord Jesus Christ.

Let us come with grateful hearts
to partake of this meal!

CHARGE

The blessing and charge may be led from the doors of the church.

May we go into the world
with the full conviction
that God is able to do
all that God has promised.
Amen. *or* **Thanks be to God.**

Proper 5

June 5–11, if after Trinity Sunday

COMPLEMENTARY READINGS

Hosea 5:15–6:6   Romans 4:13–25
Psalm 50:7–15   Matthew 9:9–13, 18–26

OPENING SENTENCES

> *¡Regresemos al Creador!* (Let us return to the Creator!)
> **For God will come to us like spring rains**
> **that give drink to the earth.**
>
> *¡Regresemos al Creador!* (Let us return to the Creator!)
> **For God will heal us and bind us up.**
>
> *¡Regresemos al Creador!* (Let us return to the Creator!)
> **For God's coming is as certain as the dawn.**

PRAYER OF THE DAY

> As sunflowers seek the sun,
> we come here seeking your face, O God.
> Hear our pleading.
> Revive us from the slumber
> of violence, greed, and willful ignorance.
> Raise us up
> like a host of sunflowers,
> ready to spread seeds of new life. **Amen.**

As Jesus was walking along, he saw a man called Matthew sitting at the tax booth; and he said to him, "Follow me." And he got up and followed him.

Matthew 9:9

INVITATION TO DISCIPLESHIP

The invitation to discipleship may be led from the baptismal font.

"Follow me," Jesus said
to an ordinary person,
knowing his crew of disciples
would be made up of ordinary people.
So Matthew got up and followed him.

Are you ready to take the first step?

PRAYERS OF INTERCESSION

The prayers of intercession may be led from the midst of the congregation.

Spring of life,
you give life to the dead.

Fill us with your love,
until we have no choice but to love
every wild animal,
all the cattle,
and all the birds of the air;
every rock,
all the oceans,
and all the trees of the forest;
every human,
from every nation,
and every culture,
and every gender expression.

Spring of life,
you call into existence
things that do not exist.

Create in us hearts that are full of compassion.
Receive our offerings of love and service.
Raise up among us bold voices to call out injustice.
Empower us to be tireless seekers of truth.
And give us strong hands
to do the work you have called us to do:
the work of love and mercy,
thanksgiving and praise.
In Jesus' name we pray. **Amen.**

INVITATION TO OFFERING

The invitation to offering may be led from the Communion table.

The Holy One does not want sacrifices
or burnt offerings,
but steadfast love and thanksgiving.

Let us offer every good gift
to the source of all things.

INVITATION TO THE TABLE

The invitation to the table is led from the Communion table.

Hoping against hope,
let us believe in God's promise
that the meal we are about to share
will be sustenance for the journey.

Let us come to this table
knowing all are welcome,
sinners and saints,
those who are well,
and those who are sick.
Let us come trusting that
in touching, and smelling,
and tasting these simple gifts
we will be made well.

CHARGE

The blessing and charge may be led from the doors of the church.

Go and learn what this means:
"I desire mercy, not sacrifice."
Take heart, for your faith will make you well.
And call on God in the day of trouble,
for God will deliver you.
Amen. *or* **Thanks be to God.**

Proper 6

June 12–18, if after Trinity Sunday

SEMICONTINUOUS READINGS

Genesis 18:1–15 (21:1–7)   Romans 5:1–8
Psalm 116:1–2, 12–19   Matthew 9:35–10:8 (9–23)

OPENING SENTENCES

> We love the Lord,
> **for God has heard us.**
>
> We return all we have to the Lord,
> **for the Lord is good.**
> **Praise the Lord!**

PRAYER OF THE DAY

> O God, we give thanks to you
> for bringing us together.
> May your Holy Spirit lead us in praising you
> so that our hearts and minds will be empowered
> to serve your people.
> In the name of Jesus Christ,
> your Son and our Savior,
> we pray. **Amen.**

INVITATION TO DISCIPLESHIP

The invitation to discipleship may be led from the baptismal font.

> "But God proves his love for us
> in that while we were still sinners
> Christ died for us."
> No matter who you are,
> God loves you.
>
> If you are called
> to be a part of this community of faith,
> we invite you to join us.

PRAYERS OF INTERCESSION

The prayers of intercession may be led from the midst of the congregation.

"I will lift up the cup of salvation
and call on the name of the Lord."
God, in your mercy,
hear our prayer.

We call on your name, O Lord,
to heal the brokenhearted . . .
Restore them to the joy of your salvation.

We call on your name, O Lord,
to restore the resources of the earth . . .
May we become better stewards of your earth,
that all will have enough.

We call on your name, O Lord,
for the well-being of our community . . .
Empower us to care for our neighbors,
as well as those we do not know.

We call on your name, O Lord,
for those who are suffering
from injustice and oppression . . .
Strengthen us for the work
of releasing others from systems
that work for a few instead of for everyone.

We call on your name, O Lord,
for those whose lives are coming to an end . . .
Assure them that nothing in life or death
can separate us from your love.

We thank you, O Lord,
for the joy of lifting up our prayers.
May we trust that you will hear
and answer according to your will.
We pray this in the name of your Son,
Jesus Christ. **Amen.**

INVITATION TO OFFERING

The invitation to offering may be led from the Communion table.

> We have plenty to offer the Lord
> for the goodness we have received.
> Let us remember
> what the Lord has done for us.
>
> Let us offer our gifts to the Lord.

INVITATION TO THE TABLE

The invitation to the table is led from the Communion table.

> Rejoice, all you people!
> The Lord is good and gracious to us.
> This is our invitation
> to partake of this meal
> that is provided for us.
> At this table
> we remember what Christ has done,
> is doing,
> and will do in our lives.
>
> Come to the feast
> that has been prepared for you!

CHARGE

The blessing and charge may be led from the doors of the church.

> Jesus said to his disciples,
> "The harvest is plentiful,
> but the laborers are few."
> Go into the world and be witnesses
> to our Lord and Savior, Jesus Christ!
> **Amen.** *or* **Thanks be to God.**

Proper 6

June 12–18, if after Trinity Sunday

COMPLEMENTARY READINGS

Exodus 19:2–8a
Psalm 100

Romans 5:1–8
Matthew 9:35–10:8 (9–23)

OPENING SENTENCES

> Because God is good:
> ***¡Canten con júbilo a nuestro Dios, toda la tierra!***
> **(Make a joyful noise to our God, all the earth!)**
>
> Because God's steadfast love endures forever:
> ***¡Canten con júbilo a nuestro Dios, toda la tierra!***
> **(Make a joyful noise to our God, all the earth!)**
>
> Because God's faithfulness lasts through all generations:
> ***¡Canten con júbilo a nuestro Dios, toda la tierra!***
> **(Make a joyful noise to our God, all the earth!)**

PRAYER OF THE DAY

> O Holy God,
> revealed to us from the mountain,
> we give thanks and bless your name.
> Make us a holy nation,
> lift us up on eagles' wings,
> and bring us to you.
> Speak and we will listen. **Amen.**

Make a joyful noise to the LORD, all the earth. Worship the LORD with gladness; come into [God's] presence with singing.

Psalm 100:1–2

INVITATION TO DISCIPLESHIP

The invitation to discipleship may be led from the baptismal font.

The soil needs to be tilled.
The seeds are ready to be planted.
The compost needs to be turned.
The harvest is plentiful,
but the laborers are few.

Come and join us.
Roll up your sleeves and show up.
Come and enjoy the bounty of God's garden.

PRAYERS OF INTERCESSION

The prayers of intercession may be led from the midst of the congregation.

Holy One,
you have called us to work:
to heal the sick
in a world where viruses create desolation
and where our obsession
with material goods and technology
devastates your good creation.
We respond to your call, saying,
"We will follow you."

You have called us to work:
to gather your sheep
in a world where we are isolated
by so many distractions—
cryptocurrencies, new devices, social influencers—
and where our desire to be perfect
alienates us from the people you made us to be.
We respond to your call, saying,
"We will follow you."

You have called us to work:
to proclaim the good news
in a world where division pervades humanity
and where our need for power
favors corporations over people.
We respond to your call, saying,
"We will follow you."

Give us all that we will need for our calling—
the wisdom of serpents
and the innocence of doves—
to speak words of compassion,
to dismantle oppressive systems,
and to believe that the kingdom of heaven is near.
Through Christ our Savior we pray. **Amen.**

INVITATION TO OFFERING

The invitation to offering may be led from the Communion table.

Just as God's love
has been poured into our hearts,
let us pour our love into the world
by sharing what we have
with this world and this community
as a sign of our hope.

Hope will not disappoint us.

INVITATION TO THE TABLE

The invitation to the table is led from the Communion table.

The harvest has been plentiful!
The laborers deserve their food!

Let us come to the table of God's bounty.

CHARGE

The blessing and charge may be led from the doors of the church.

Go and proclaim the good news:
"The kingdom of heaven has come near."
Cure the sick, raise the dead,
cleanse the lepers, cast out demons,
for the Spirit of your Heavenly Parent
will be speaking through you.
Amen. *or* **Thanks be to God.**

Proper 7

June 19–25, if after Trinity Sunday

SEMICONTINUOUS READINGS

Genesis 21:8–21   Romans 6:1b–11
Psalm 86:1–10, 16–17   Matthew 10:24–39

OPENING SENTENCES

> When Abraham was troubled,
> **God said, "Do not be distressed."**
>
> When Hagar gave up,
> **God said, "Do not be afraid."**
>
> No matter what happens,
> **God is with us. Praise the Lord!**

PRAYER OF THE DAY

> Loving God,
> you reveal your presence in our lives.
> Renew our hearts and minds
> through the power of the Holy Spirit,
> that we may worship you in truth and spirit.
> We ask this in the name
> of your Son and our Savior,
> Jesus Christ. **Amen.**

INVITATION TO DISCIPLESHIP

The invitation to discipleship may be led from the baptismal font.

> Jesus continually calls us
> into a relationship with him.
>
> If you are ready to make a commitment
> to follow Christ, we invite you.
> We welcome you.

PRAYERS OF INTERCESSION

The prayers of intercession may be led from the midst of the congregation.

As we gather in this community of faith,
we lift up our prayers to God
for ourselves and others.

We pray for the church . . .
May you bless and guide
each community of faith
to be your hands and feet in the world.

We pray for our elected leaders . . .
Give them wisdom from your Holy Spirit
to follow your will and way
for the benefit of all people.

We pray for those who are ill and homebound . . .
Help them know your healing presence,
that they may be restored.

We pray for pastors . . .
Strengthen them in the proclamation of your Word,
and bless their loved ones.

We pray for broken relationships . . .
Restore our shattered hearts and minds,
and assure us of your healing powers.

We ask for these and other blessings
in the name of your Son, Jesus Christ. **Amen.**

INVITATION TO OFFERING

The invitation to offering may be led from the Communion table.

The Lord is good and gracious,
abounding in steadfast love.
The Lord is the giver of all things;
we respond with gratitude.

Let us offer our lives to the Lord.

INVITATION TO THE TABLE

The invitation to the table is led from the Communion table.

> Our Lord invites you to this feast,
> which has been prepared for you
> through the gracious mercy of God
> and the life, death, and resurrection
> of Jesus Christ.
>
> Come, one and all, to the table.

CHARGE

The blessing and charge may be led from the doors of the church.

> Beloved, no matter where you go,
> may you live in the assurance
> that God is present with you always.
> **Amen.** *or* **Thanks be to God.**

Proper 7

June 19–25, if after Trinity Sunday

COMPLEMENTARY READINGS

Jeremiah 20:7–13   Romans 6:1b–11
Psalm 69:7–10 (11–15), 16–18   Matthew 10:24–39

OPENING SENTENCES

> Sing to our God; praise our God!
> **Even when we become strangers
> to our own families.**
>
> Sing to our God; praise our God!
> **Even when we are the subject of gossip.**
>
> Sing to our God; praise our God!
> **For God is our strong defender.**
>
> Sing to our God; praise our God!
> **For God will deliver us from the deep waters.**
>
> Sing to our God; praise our God!
> **For God's steadfast love is good.**

PRAYER OF THE DAY

> Holy, triune God,
> as we remember our baptism—
> water, death, resurrection,
> dove, fire, Spirit—
> help us remember that
> death is not the end,
> that we will walk in newness of life
> with Christ,
> through Christ,
> and in Christ. **Amen.**

INVITATION TO DISCIPLESHIP

The invitation to discipleship may be led from the baptismal font.

God calls us to be prophets,
messengers of God's peace and justice
to this world.
It is like a burning fire within each of us,
a force that moves us
to act with compassion,
a voice that comes from a place
deeper than our minds.

Listen to the voice calling; it is there.
God will be with you each step of the way.

PRAYERS OF INTERCESSION

The prayers of intercession may be led from the midst of the congregation.

Fire in our bones,
you have called people
from every time and place
to speak your words.

We give thanks for those
who prophesy to your people,
even when they are fearful
and rejected by society.

We give thanks for those
who have been mocked,
rejected by their families
because of zeal for your house.

We give thanks for those
who have lost their lives,
figuratively and literally,
for speaking the truth.

We give thanks for those
who have taken up their cross
knowing the price to pay was high
but the price of silence was even higher.

Spark the fire of your Word in our hearts,
that we may be bold and fearless
as messengers of your good news.
Draw near to us when we feel lonely.
Redeem us when we face injustice.
Set us free when we are oppressed.
In Jesus' name we pray. **Amen.**

INVITATION TO OFFERING

The invitation to offering may be led from the Communion table.

We have been set free
so we can set others free.
We have been given new life
so we can bring new life to others.
We have been blessed abundantly
so we can bless others.

Let us give thanks by sharing our gifts
with the one who sets us free,
gives us new life,
and blesses us abundantly.

INVITATION TO THE TABLE

The invitation to the table is led from the Communion table.

We come to the mystery of this table
with questions and doubts,
with broken hearts and fear.
But we also come knowing
that our brokenness and our wholeness
will become known,
that we will become fully known
and we will be enough.
We come to this table knowing
that nothing is covered up
that will not be uncovered,
and nothing is secret
that will not be made known.

Come, taste and see.

CHARGE

The blessing and charge may be led from the doors of the church.

Go and be messengers of God's justice.
Do not be afraid as you follow Jesus.
We will find life.
For the creator of us all
will be with us until the end of time.
Amen. *or* **Thanks be to God.**

Proper 8

June 26–July 2

SEMICONTINUOUS READINGS

Genesis 22:1–14   Romans 6:12–23
Psalm 13   Matthew 10:40–42

OPENING SENTENCES

> We trust in your steadfast love;
> **our hearts shall rejoice in your salvation.**
>
> The Lord has dealt charitably with us.
> **Praise the Lord!**

PRAYER OF THE DAY

> O God,
> you are truly worthy to be praised,
> for you are gracious,
> compassionate, and merciful.
> Send your Holy Spirit among us,
> that we may hear your voice
> and praise your name
> this day and forevermore. **Amen.**

INVITATION TO DISCIPLESHIP

The invitation to discipleship may be led from the baptismal font.

> "Whoever welcomes you welcomes me,
> and whoever welcomes me
> welcomes the one who sent me."
>
> As followers of Jesus Christ,
> we want to welcome you
> into this community of faith.
> If you are ready and willing,
> we are here to receive you.

PRAYERS OF INTERCESSION

The prayers of intercession may be led from the midst of the congregation.

Faithful God, we are thankful
that we always have the opportunity
to cast our joys and concerns upon you.
Hear us now as we pray:
God of mercy, **hear our prayer.**

We pray for those who are sick
and facing serious illness . . .
God of mercy, **hear our prayer.**

We pray for those who are lost
and seek direction . . .
God of mercy, **hear our prayer.**

We pray for the governments of every land . . .
God of mercy, **hear our prayer.**

We pray for churches throughout the world . . .
God of mercy, **hear our prayer.**

We pray for those who have suffered
from natural disasters . . .
God of mercy, **hear our prayer.**

We pray for those who live in our community . . .
God of mercy, **hear our prayer.**

We pray, O God, that you will hear
and answer our prayers in due time.
Until then, keep us steadfast in our faith.
We ask this in the name of your Son,
Jesus Christ. **Amen.**

INVITATION TO OFFERING

The invitation to offering may be led from the Communion table.

Jesus says, "It is more blessed
to give than to receive."

With gratitude to God,
let us receive the offering,
returning to God
the gifts we have been given.

INVITATION TO THE TABLE

The invitation to the table is led from the Communion table.

We praise you, O God,
for setting a place for us at this table.
We are here
not by our own strength or worthiness.
It is only through your grace
that a place is made for us.

Come, take your place at this table,
and let us give thanks to God.

CHARGE

The blessing and charge may be led from the doors of the church.

Go from this place to serve the Lord
this day and forevermore.
Amen. *or* **Thanks be to God.**

Proper 8

June 26–July 2

COMPLEMENTARY READINGS

Jeremiah 28:5–9   Romans 6:12–23

Psalm 89:1–4, 15–18   Matthew 10:40–42

OPENING SENTENCES

> Because your steadfast love is eternal,
> **we will sing of your love to all generations!**
>
> Because your faithfulness is as firm as the heavens,
> **we will sing of your love to all generations!**
>
> Because you are our strength and our shield,
> **we will sing of your love to all generations!**
>
> Let us worship the Holy One of Israel!

PRAYER OF THE DAY

> Fountain of grace and eternal life,
> help us live a holy life—
> one in which we are instruments of your will
> and sin does not have power over us—
> for you have brought us from death to life,
> and you have taught us the way of love. **Amen.**

INVITATION TO DISCIPLESHIP

The invitation to discipleship may be led from the baptismal font.

> The Holy One,
> who gathers together
> all those who have lived in exile,
> invites us all
> to be prophets of peace,
> instruments of peace,
> builders of peace.

This invitation is extended
to all who hope for peace.

Will you join us in this holy work?

PRAYERS OF INTERCESSION

The prayers of intercession may be led from the midst of the congregation.

God of extravagant welcome,
day after day you ask us to welcome you—
by welcoming the prophets,
by welcoming the righteous,
by giving a cup of cold water
to one who is thirsty.

Help us open our doors and hearts
to wanderers and wonderers . . .

to those who are wise
and those who are foolish . . .

to those who are thirsty
and those who are hungry . . .

to those who are tired
and those who have nowhere else to go . . .

to those who knock on our door
and those who run away from it . . .

God of extravagant welcome,
help us to understand that
in welcoming one and all,
we welcome you.
Teach us your way of welcome
so we can live in the hope
that you will welcome us
to your dwelling place
and to the holy feast
and to you yourself;
through Christ our Savior. **Amen.**

INVITATION TO OFFERING

The invitation to offering may be led from the Communion table.

We give thanks and praise
for God our strength and shield
and for every blessing
that comes from God.

Let us share what we have
with thanksgiving,
and with a joyful shout.

INVITATION TO THE TABLE

The invitation to the table is led from the Communion table.

"Welcome me," says God—
while Holy Love
sets the table,
prepares a spread,
kneads bread,
crushes grapes,
and patiently waits
for the yeast
to raise the bread,
to ferment the wine,
and to raise all of us
from death to life.

You are welcome here.

CHARGE

The blessing and charge may be led from the doors of the church.

Now go from this place
to speak words of peace,
to sing of God's love and faithfulness,
to welcome everyone with open arms,
and to serve the one who has made you holy.
Amen. *or* **Thanks be to God.**

Proper 9

July 3–9

SEMICONTINUOUS READINGS

Genesis 24:34–38,   Romans 7:15–25a
  42–49, 58–67   Matthew 11:16–19, 25–30
Psalm 45:10–17 *or*
  Song of Solomon 2:8–13

OPENING SENTENCES

> We gather around the well of Beer-lahai-roi,
> the place where God sees us.
> **We gather to see and be seen.**
> **To know and be known.**
> **To behold and be held.**
>
> We thirst and drink deeply
> from these living waters.

PRAYER OF THE DAY

> God, you know our deepest griefs
> and our highest hopes.
> Meet us in this moment,
> and help us to open ourselves
> to your work of healing and transformation.
> Let your Spirit move freely,
> not only in this space,
> but in every corner of our lives.
> Equip us to embody
> your grace and courage,
> for the sake of Christ our Savior. **Amen.**

"Before I had finished speaking in my heart, there was Rebekah coming out with her water jar on her shoulder; and she went down to the spring, and drew. I said, 'Please let me drink.'"

Genesis 24:45

INVITATION TO DISCIPLESHIP

The invitation to discipleship may be led from the baptismal font.

God is gracious and merciful,
slow to anger and abounding in love.
God's goodness and compassion
cloaks our very being.
No matter where you have been
or what you have done,
no matter where you are going
or how you have shown up today,
you are invited to enter this mercy,
compassion, and abundant love.

Will you receive this gift today?
How will you let it transform your very being
so that others might know
the same kind of restorative grace?

PRAYERS OF INTERCESSION

The prayers of intercession may be led from the midst of the congregation.

As we enter into prayer today,
let us lift up all of those people and places,
circumstances and situations
that demand an uncommon hope today.

We pray for our world . . .

We pray for our neighbors . . .

We pray for this community . . .

We pray for our deepest concerns . . .

Jesus, you come to us
triumphant and humble,
victorious and peaceful.
Help us to be prisoners and proclaimers
of an uncommon hope.

Call us to a higher possibility—
as agents of restorative justice,
carrying forward the transforming work of grace
that we have received from ancestors of the faith.
In your holy name we pray. **Amen.**

INVITATION TO OFFERING

The invitation to offering may be led from the Communion table.

The lives we lead are not our own.
They are inextricably entwined
with the lives of those around us.
We give not as payment but as offering—
to God, to this community, and to ourselves.
We define ourselves not by our net worth,
but by the measure of God's infinite love.

And so as we give,
let us give with a gratitude and generosity
that reflects our faith in God's love.

INVITATION TO THE TABLE

The invitation to the table is led from the Communion table.

We come to this table
carrying the heavy burdens of life and living,
and before we take our seat,
Jesus invites us to lay them down
so that we might truly enjoy the meal.

This is a table where we are expected to feast
on the richness of faith and love
and on a story that is still being written.
We dine not as individuals,
but as members of a community
spanning space and time,
with those who have gathered
around tables like this one
since the early days of the church.

With these ancestors of the faith we pray.

The Great Thanksgiving continues . . .

CHARGE

The blessing and charge may be led from the doors of the church.

Go forth from this place
with your burdens lightened—
not only by the nourishment of spirit
that you have been given,
but by the strength of knowing
your burdens are shared
in Christian community.
Go forth to be God's voice of grace
wherever you find yourself in the days to come.
Amen. *or* **Thanks be to God.**

Proper 9

July 3–9

COMPLEMENTARY READINGS

Zechariah 9:9–12
Psalm 145:8–14

Romans 7:15–25a
Matthew 11:16–19, 25–30

OPENING SENTENCES

> Rejoice, O people! Shout aloud!
> **The God of compassion calls us together!**
>
> The day of peace is here,
> and the time for singing has come.
> **Here we find God's wisdom,**
> **God's love,**
> **God's abundance,**
> **waiting for us.**

PRAYER OF THE DAY

> Holy One,
> we meet you here today,
> seeking your revelation,
> seeking your forgiveness,
> seeking your will.
> Delight us with your presence,
> so we may eagerly learn from you. **Amen.**

INVITATION TO DISCIPLESHIP

The invitation to discipleship may be led from the baptismal font.

> Christ is the one who rescues us,
> saving us from our cycles of sin
> and bestowing on us a yoke that is easy
> and a burden that is light.
>
> What do you need to set aside this week?
> How is God disrupting your life today?

PRAYERS OF INTERCESSION

The prayers of intercession may be led from the midst of the congregation.

Holy One, hear our prayer.

For those who do good—
who help others without thought of their own gain,
who listen to those whom others refuse to hear,
who share with those who have less,
who stand up for the dignity of all people.
May they be blessed with courage and strength
to continue to be your hands and feet in the world.

For those who do ill—
who seek their own advancement at the expense of others,
who refuse to acknowledge the harm they do,
who hoard resources,
who deny the humanity of those unlike them.
May their point of view expand,
so they may see the pain they cause and truly repent.

For those of us who try to do good
but too often end up doing ill—
who try to change but slip into old habits,
who help others but only when it is convenient,
who seek justice as long as there is no sacrifice,
who love our neighbors but love ourselves more.
May we be guided by your grace and mercy,
leading us back to your way and your truth. **Amen.**

INVITATION TO OFFERING

The invitation to offering may be led from the Communion table.

God has given us a myriad of gifts:
energy, companionship, possessions, time.

Each in our own way,
let us return a portion of our blessings back to God.

INVITATION TO THE TABLE

The invitation to the table is led from the Communion table.

Here it is: the table of rest.
Here it is: the table of renewal.
Jesus invites us, calling,
"Come to me!
Lay down your burdens."

This table is food for the hungry.
This table is hope for the weary.
Here it is: the joyful feast of Jesus Christ.

CHARGE

The blessing and charge may be led from the doors of the church.

Go and sin no more!
We will, with God's help.
Amen. *or* **Thanks be to God.**

Proper 10

July 10–16

SEMICONTINUOUS READINGS

Genesis 25:19–34   Romans 8:1–11
Psalm 119:105–112   Matthew 13:1–9, 18–23

OPENING SENTENCES

> We come to remember.
> **We come to learn.**
>
> We come to offer praise.
> **We come to live in God's truth,**
> **to hold fast to God's laws,**
> **and to rejoice in God's word.**

PRAYER OF THE DAY

> O Wisdom,
> we strive to follow your word
> but often gather as unruly siblings,
> with petty fights and concerns distracting us.
> As you draw us together,
> hold us in your Spirit of righteousness and unity,
> so we might set our minds on you. **Amen.**

INVITATION TO DISCIPLESHIP

The invitation to discipleship may be led from the baptismal font.

> Scripture teaches us
> that there is no condemnation in Jesus Christ.
> Wherever you have been
> and wherever you are headed,
> you are not far from God's liberating grace
> through Jesus Christ.
>
> You are invited to experience this freedom
> so that others might also know
> the emancipation of God's restorative love.

PRAYERS OF INTERCESSION

The prayers of intercession may be led from the midst of the congregation.

God, your word is a lamp to our feet
and a light to our path.
Our world is filled with uncertainty
in nearly every corner of life and living.
We know that this does not escape your notice,
even as you call us to lift our gaze
to the greater work that you are doing.
So as we lift up our petitions,
incline your ear to hear about our burdens,
and incline our hearts to embody your principles
in response to every circumstance and situation:

We pray for our world . . .

We pray for our neighbors . . .

We pray for this community . . .

We pray for our deepest concerns . . .

Loving and liberating God,
loosen all that binds us,
so that we might find our next steps in your light
and the world may see our answered prayers
in the actions that you invite us to take. **Amen.**

INVITATION TO OFFERING

The invitation to offering may be led from the Communion table.

Ours is a God of abundance,
who created a world where all can be nourished
to fullness and thriving.
As partners in creation,
we are tasked to participate in this work of nourishment
in whatever ways and by whatever means we can.

As we receive our financial offering today,
let us understand it as one way
in which we claim God's abundance
and carry it forward as cocreators and partners
in God's vision of wholeness of life for all.

INVITATION TO THE TABLE

The invitation to the table is led from the Communion table.

We come to this table aware of all the ways
that we thirst and hunger for God's restorative work
within and among us.
As we take our place at the table,
we remember that the ways in which
we suffer and cause suffering
need not be the final chapters of our stories.
For when we dine at God's table,
we feast alongside so many others
who have also grappled with the ways
they have not lived up to God's highest ideals.
We remember that our invitation
is not contingent upon our actions,
but upon our willingness to show up
and receive the welcome of God
and her saints across space and time.

Let us gather at this table.

CHARGE

The blessing and charge may be led from the doors of the church.

Go to the world,
walking in the way of God's word.
Amen. *or* **Thanks be to God.**

Proper 10

July 10–16

COMPLEMENTARY READINGS

Isaiah 55:10–13
Psalm 65:(1–8) 9–13

Romans 8:1–11
Matthew 13:1–9, 18–23

OPENING SENTENCES

Happy are those
who dwell near to God's courts!
**Let us draw near to God,
our source of goodness and joy,
our salvation and our hope.**

PRAYER OF THE DAY

O God, who sows the seeds of our faith,
till the soil of our hearts and minds
so that what you plant might be nurtured
into fullness of life;
for the sake of Christ our Savior. **Amen.**

INVITATION TO DISCIPLESHIP

The invitation to discipleship may be led from the baptismal font.

There is no condemnation for those
who dwell with the Spirit of God,
for the Spirit is life and peace.

If you seek that Spirit of righteousness,
if your soul longs for that freedom, come.

> *There is therefore now no condemnation for those who are
> in Christ Jesus. For the law of the Spirit of life in Christ
> Jesus has set you free from the law of sin and of death.*
>
> *Romans 8:1–2*

PRAYERS OF INTERCESSION

The prayers of intercession may be led from the midst of the congregation.

O God, we pray for the seeds that fall
on every kind of soil.

For those who fall on the path,
where they are vulnerable and isolated,
we pray for protection and companionship.

For those who fall on rocky ground,
where they do not have the resources they need,
we pray for support and resilience.

For those who fall among thorns,
where oppressive forces knock them down,
we pray for strength and deliverance.

For those who fall in good soil,
where they are given all they need,
we pray for humility and generosity.

God of the harvest,
let good things grow among us
until that day when you gather us up
in your realm of righteousness and peace;
through Jesus Christ our Savior. **Amen.**

INVITATION TO OFFERING

The invitation to offering may be led from the Communion table.

We have been given life,
so let us live our lives in gratitude.

We have been given salvation,
so let us live our lives in peace.

We have been given abundance,
so let us live our lives in gratitude.

INVITATION TO THE TABLE

The invitation to the table is led from the Communion table.

This table is the garden—
a place for nurture and care,
a place where the soil is healthy and good,
where our roots stretch deep
and our leaves reach gratefully toward the sun.

Come and be nourished here,
so we might bear fruit
beyond our wildest imaginings.

CHARGE

The blessing and charge may be led from the doors of the church.

Go forward from this place
freed from condemnation,
empowered for transformation,
and inspired for restoration
wherever you go in the days to come.
Amen. *or* **Thanks be to God.**

Proper 11

July 17–23

SEMICONTINUOUS READINGS

Genesis 28:10–19a
Psalm 139:1–12, 23–24

Romans 8:12–25
Matthew 13:24–30, 36–43

OPENING SENTENCES

How awesome is this place!
This is none other than the house of God.
**Let this moment and this space
be a gateway to wholeness of life for all!**

PRAYER OF THE DAY

God who knows us completely,
who knows our words
before we even have a chance to speak,
wrap us in your presence.
Still the distractions that well up in us.
Search us, know us,
and guide us to the wisdom
you would have us hear today. **Amen.**

---

*Where can I go from your spirit? Or where can I flee
from your presence? If I ascend to heaven, you are there;
if I make my bed in Sheol, you are there.*

Psalm 139:7–8

INVITATION TO DISCIPLESHIP

The invitation to discipleship may be led from the baptismal font.

God has searched us and knows us.
She is acquainted with all of our ways.
While there may be parts of ourselves
that we wish were not,
that we have worked to keep hidden,
there is no place to which we can flee
that will be out of reach for God's grace.

You are invited in this moment
to relax into the grace of the one
who knows and loves our whole selves,
and who liberates us from everything
that would tell us we are less.
Accept this invitation,
and find yourself made complete in God's love.

PRAYERS OF INTERCESSION

The prayers of intercession may be led from the midst of the congregation.

God of strength and of peace,
of power and of grace,
we come before you this day
with hearts full and hearts heavy,
uplifted by dreams
and weighed down by nightmares.
Meet us in this space,
and hear us as we bring before you
those circumstances, people, and possibilities
that rest heavily on our hearts.

For those who struggle with illness
of heart, mind, and body,
we seek healing, helping, and compassion . . .

For those communities seeking resources
to achieve the basic services
that allow for peace and connection,
we seek justice, equity, and abundance . . .

For those leaders who make decisions
on behalf of people in different contexts,
we seek critical engagement,
opportunities for connection,
and courage to lead with imagination . . .

God of enough,
you have shown strength and generosity
to those who doubt the completeness of your power
and misunderstand the purpose of your practices.
Help us to be people
who walk not only with confidence
but also with commitment
to your vision of wholeness of life for all.
Help us to take action
for the sake of this vision,
of one another,
and of the whole creation
you have entrusted to our care. **Amen.**

INVITATION TO OFFERING

The invitation to offering may be led from the Communion table.

God is with us.
God keeps us wherever we go.
God does not leave us with unfulfilled promises.

Let these gifts be our pillars of stone,
our oil poured out
in gratitude for all God does for us.

INVITATION TO THE TABLE

The invitation to the table is led from the Communion table.

This is the family table.
It is big enough for all to sit together.
It is big enough to hold our similarities and our differences,
our arguments and our agreements.
It is a glimpse of what the world will look like
when all creation is freed from greed and exploitation
and we are truly united as children of God.

Come. Witness. Feast. Celebrate.

CHARGE

The blessing and charge may be led from the doors of the church.

As you leave this space,
do not be discouraged by the weeds
that may grow around you.
Know that God sees you, sustains you,
and supplies you with what you need
to pursue wholeness of life for all.
Amen. *or* **Thanks be to God.**

Proper 11

July 17–23

COMPLEMENTARY READINGS

Wisdom 12:13, 16–19
  or Isaiah 44:6–8
Psalm 86:11–17

Romans 8:12–25
Matthew 13:24–30, 36–43

OPENING SENTENCES

We come from north, south,
east, and west, proclaiming:
Great is the steadfast love of God!

We are brought together—
a widespread, diverse family, rejoicing:
Great is the steadfast love of God!

PRAYER OF THE DAY

O God, our great redeemer,
enable us to see your activity among us,
that even as we live in a world
filled with anxiety and scarcity,
we might live with the assurance
of your abundant promise
of protection and grace, and the promise
that you will never leave us nor forsake us;
for the sake of Christ our Savior. **Amen.**

INVITATION TO DISCIPLESHIP

The invitation to discipleship may be led from the baptismal font.

If we are honest,
we know that we can bear good fruit,
but we struggle with the weeds
that grow up around our hearts.

What are the weeds you are facing today?
How can you nurture the fruit of good works within you?

PRAYERS OF INTERCESSION

The prayers of intercession may be led from the midst of the congregation.

The glory that will one day be revealed to us
may be tremendous,
but the sufferings of this present time weigh on us.

We wait with longing:

for creation to be restored . . .

for the sick to be healed . . .

for the oppressed to receive justice . . .

for the lonely to be seen . . .

for the ruthless to find compassion . . .

for the neglected to receive care . . .

for the violent to put down their weapons . . .

for the weary to find strength . . .

O Savior, we hope for what we do not yet see.
Help us to wait for it with patience;
in your holy name we pray. **Amen.**

INVITATION TO OFFERING

The invitation to offering may be led from the Communion table.

As we continue our worship
through the receiving of financial offerings,
let us all remember that
while we live in a world shaped by transactions,
God's economy is one of gifts freely offered.

Let us share our financial gifts
as a sign of our participation in and allegiance to
a new way of life and being—
one that is rooted in the understanding
that our life together is enriched
by the offerings we render to God and one another.

INVITATION TO THE TABLE

The invitation to the table is led from the Communion table.

This table is a harvest;
the place where God's good seeds—
sown with love and care
over centuries and across generations
and in every corner of the earth—
have taken root, weathered seasons,
and faithfully borne fruit with every passing year.
It is the place where we receive sustenance
from the efforts of those who came before us.
It is where we dine with them
and are encouraged by them,
remembering that we do not walk alone
as we seek to live lives
shaped and guided by God's grace.

Come to this table.

CHARGE

The blessing and charge may be led from the doors of the church.

Go forth with hope;
in hope we are saved.
Amen. *or* **Thanks be to God.**

Proper 12

July 24–30

SEMICONTINUOUS READINGS

Genesis 29:15–28
Psalm 105:1–11, 45b
  or Psalm 128

Romans 8:26–39
Matthew 13:31–33, 44–52

OPENING SENTENCES

> O give thanks to God!
> **Remember the wonderful things God has done!**
>
> Glory in God's holy name!
> **Sing of God's acts and promises!**
>
> We will seek God's presence;
> **let the hearts of those who seek God rejoice.**

PRAYER OF THE DAY

> God of our ancestors,
> you have always been faithful to us,
> keeping your promises to us,
> even when we have not kept our promises to you.
> As we praise you this day,
> guide us into new understandings
> of your love for us
> and of the kin-dom you call us to be. **Amen.**

[Jesus] put before them another parable: "The kingdom of heaven is like a mustard seed that someone took and sowed in his field; it is the smallest of all the seeds, but when it has grown it is the greatest of shrubs and becomes a tree, so that the birds of the air come and make nests in its branches."

Matthew 13:31–32

INVITATION TO DISCIPLESHIP

The invitation to discipleship may be led from the baptismal font.

Scripture shows us there is no condemnation in Christ Jesus,
who invites us into deep restoration and relationship.
For there is nothing—
neither death, nor life,
nor angels, nor rulers,
nor things present, nor things to come,
nor powers, nor height, nor depth,
nor anything else in all creation—
that can separate us from God's love.

Receive this relationship
and experience the transformative power of this love.
Let it renew your heart,
your relationships,
and the world around you.

PRAYERS OF INTERCESSION

The prayers of intercession may be led from the midst of the congregation.

O God, we do not always have the words
to speak aloud what weighs heaviest on our hearts.
And yet even in this you provide for us,
sending your Spirit to intercede on our behalf.
Hear our prayers in this moment.

For those seeking peace amid chaotic circumstances,
whose lives are filled with hardship or distress,
persecution or hunger,
vulnerability, oppression, or danger,
we pray protection, power, and perseverance . . .

For those who perpetuate and benefit from oppression,
whose lives have been carefully crafted
to shelter them from the pain of others,
we pray inbreaking, upsetting,
and restoration of connection to you and to one another . . .

For those whose mustard-seed-sized faith
has been stretched as far as it could go,
we ask your grace and courage . . .

For all of us,
as we navigate our way through a world
without clear pathways forward or clear options,
help us to have the wisdom
to choose what is faithful over what is convenient,
what is life-giving instead of what is self-serving,
what is nourishing rather than what distracts . . .

O God,
who searches our hearts and knows our minds,
we trust and believe
that all things work together for good
for those who love you
and who are called according to your purpose.
Let us participate in this good work and true purpose
for the sake of all creation. **Amen.**

INVITATION TO OFFERING

The invitation to offering may be led from the Communion table.

When we offer our lives for God's transforming work,
we embody a new way of understanding who we are—
as a people in connection to one another
and deeply invested in the work that God is doing
with all the gifts that we have been given.

As you offer your gifts in this time,
let it be from a spirit of generosity, joy, and expectation,
that we might be part of the transformation
we seek in the world.

INVITATION TO THE TABLE

The invitation to the table is led from the Communion table.

> Jesus teaches us that the kin-dom of heaven
> is as common as a bit of yeast or a merchant,
> a treasure buried in a field or a net thrown into the sea,
> a pearl of great value or a table set for all ages.
> God's presence among us is wholly ordinary,
> even as it is extraordinary.
> We gather in the company that Jesus kept—
> wealthy elites and lonely outcasts,
> children who dared to tell the truth
> and widows endlessly seeking justice.
>
> In the good company of these ancestors in faith,
> let us come to the table.

CHARGE

The blessing and charge may be led from the doors of the church.

> Go forth from this place,
> knowing that your fragile faith
> will be enough to get you through this day
> and the days to come,
> believing that God will do more with your faith
> than you could ever imagine.
> **Amen.** *or* **Thanks be to God.**

Proper 12

July 24–30

COMPLEMENTARY READINGS

1 Kings 3:5–12

Psalm 119:129–136

Romans 8:26–39

Matthew 13:31–33, 44–52

OPENING SENTENCES

Turn to us and be gracious, O God,
for we love your holy name.

Keep our steps steady, according to your promise,
and never let evil have dominion over us.

Redeem us from oppression,
that we may keep your commandments.

Let your face shine upon us,
and teach us your way of life.

PRAYER OF THE DAY

O God, whose words light our way,
illumine our hearts and minds
as we encounter you this day.
Help us to be present in all the ways
that allow us to enter into your transformative grace,
so that when we leave
we might be made more whole,
more courageous,
and more connected
to one another in your love;
for the sake of Christ our Savior. **Amen.**

INVITATION TO DISCIPLESHIP

The invitation to discipleship may be led from the baptismal font.

All of us are called
by the one who died for us,
who justifies and glorifies us
to live according to God's love.

How is God nudging you to live out your call this week?
What do you feel is blocking you from that call?
What might it look like to move past those obstacles,
knowing that nothing can separate you from Christ's love?

PRAYERS OF INTERCESSION

The prayers of intercession may be led from the midst of the congregation.

God of small and great,
of simple and wise,
of things treasured and forgotten,
hear our prayer.

We pray for small things—
the seed that grows into a bountiful plant,
the idea that becomes a ministry,
the get-well note that arrives
at the moment when it is sorely needed.

We pray for simple things—
the home-cooked meal given to a grieving family,
the short conversation with someone
who doesn't get out much,
the energy of volunteer work
to lighten another's load.

We pray for treasured things—
the long-awaited reunions,
the sincerely given apologies
and generous forgiveness,
the safety of a community
where we are known and loved.

We pray that we might be bearers
of these small, simple, treasured things,
that through them
your love and care may be known to all;
through Jesus Christ our Savior. **Amen.**

INVITATION TO OFFERING

The invitation to offering may be led from the Communion table.

God treasures our lives.
God treasures our faith, even when it seems tiny.
God treasures our prayers.
God treasures our worship.
God treasures our very beings.
All we have is a reflection of God's glory.

Now let us respond to that generosity
by returning a portion of the treasures we have been given
back to God's work in this world.

INVITATION TO THE TABLE

The invitation to the table is led from the Communion table.

There is nothing that can separate us
from the love of God in Christ Jesus.
Not death or life,
not what has happened in the past
or what will happen in the future,
nothing we have done or failed to do.
Nothing.

This table is where we give thanks for that love,
the strongest force we know.
This table is where we gather to remember
that we are recipients of that boundless love.
This table is where we celebrate
that God's love has the final word.

CHARGE

The blessing and charge may be led from the doors of the church.

Go into the world to live the life
to which you were called.
Praise be to Jesus Christ!
Amen. *or* **Thanks be to God.**

Proper 13

July 31–August 6

SEMICONTINUOUS READINGS

Genesis 32:22–31   Romans 9:1–5
Psalm 17:1–7, 15   Matthew 14:13–21

OPENING SENTENCES

In this place,
in this time of worship,
we feel the presence of God.

In our words,
in our song,
we sing the beauty of God.

In each person,
in each soul,
we see the face of God.

PRAYER OF THE DAY

O God, who calls us to healing and wholeness,
prepare our hearts to receive your invitation of restoration—
with you, with one another, and with ourselves.
Let this time in which we gather
be the space where we can wrestle
with our questions and our pain,
even as we find assurance in your presence and power;
for the sake of Christ our Savior. **Amen.**

---

*Jacob was left alone; and a man
wrestled with him until daybreak.*

Genesis 32:24

INVITATION TO DISCIPLESHIP

The invitation to discipleship may be led from the baptismal font.

God does not require us
to have everything figured out before we follow.
God meets us where we are
and wrestles with us,
challenges us,
and blesses us.

What are you wrestling with in your faith today?
How can you use that struggle to move forward in faith?

PRAYERS OF INTERCESSION

The prayers of intercession may be led from the midst of the congregation.

God who is present,
God who is with us,
God who cared about us so much
that you came to be with us:
we yearn for your goodwill.
With the insistence of Jacob,
we ask for your blessing.

We ask for your blessing on this earth—
on the land that cries out from exploitation,
on the waters that struggle with pollution,
on the skies that scorch us with unprecedented heat.

We ask for your blessing on humanity—
on those who are treated unfairly,
on those in the midst of violence and destruction,
on those who are most affected by climate disasters.

We ask for your blessing on our community—
on the ministries of this church,
on those who cannot be with us today,
on those neighbors we seek to serve.

We ask for your blessing on our friends and family—
on those who are sick or grieving,
on those who are celebrating new life and opportunity,
on those who are struggling to get by.

We ask for your blessing
knowing that you are generous and gracious.
We ask for your blessing
knowing that you are the God of our past, present,
and future.
We ask for your blessing
knowing that you are the source of all life.
Hear our prayer. **Amen.**

INVITATION TO OFFERING

The invitation to offering may be led from the Communion table.

We know what God can do
with the smallest offering.
We know that God transforms our gifts
into abundance for all in need.

Trusting in this miracle,
we offer what we have now.

INVITATION TO THE TABLE

The invitation to the table is led from the Communion table.

When we are scared that there will not be enough—
that the need is too overwhelming,
that we cannot muster the energy
or the resources to do what must be done—
that is when we should gather here,
at God's table.

Christ's table is set with plenty.
There is always enough to go around.
What we bring is enough,
because Christ uses it in ways we could never imagine.
Let us remember that in Christ
there is always enough.

CHARGE

The blessing and charge may be led from the doors of the church.

Go to speak the truth in Christ!
Amen. *or* **Thanks be to God.**

Proper 13

July 31—August 6

COMPLEMENTARY READINGS

Isaiah 55:1–5   Romans 9:1–5
Psalm 145:8–9, 14–21   Matthew 14:13–21

OPENING SENTENCES

All who are thirsty,
come to the living waters of God.
All who are hungry,
gather around the bread of life.
Quench your thirst and eat your fill.

Let your spirit be nourished
by God's provision,
and let your heart be satisfied
with God's good work!

PRAYER OF THE DAY

God of grace and mercy,
we call on you, knowing you will answer.
Show us your steadfast love.
As we gather together,
give us our food in due season,
and satisfy the desire of every living being,
that we might know more fully
what it is to be your people. **Amen.**

INVITATION TO DISCIPLESHIP

The invitation to discipleship may be led from the baptismal font.

Jesus invites us all to see
that ours is a world where there is enough:
enough love, enough resources,
enough connection, and enough self-worth.

You are invited into this way of being:
one in which we are no longer
threatened by the tyranny of scarcity
but blessed by the generosity of abundance.
Receive this invitation and find liberation
from anxiety, fear, and suspicion.

PRAYERS OF INTERCESSION

The prayers of intercession may be led from the midst of the congregation.

God of enough, we confess to you
that we too often believe the myths of scarcity
that keep us pitted against one another.
Forgive our fragile and fearful mind-sets,
and replace them with attitudes of trust and abundance.
Let us be people who enable your whole creation to thrive.
As we lift up the circumstances and situations
that weigh heavily on our minds,
let us also be stirred to meet those prayers
with actions that support our petitions.

For places where war and injustice
threaten the possibility of peace,
we seek deliverance from violence and oppression . . .

For those decision makers
who shape the lives of ordinary people,
we seek wisdom, compassion, and perspective . . .

For those whose lives are shaped by decision makers,
we seek courage to speak up
and connection to care for one another . . .

For our economic systems,
which thrive on a sense of scarcity,
we seek mutuality and sustainability . . .

For our worldviews and imaginations,
we seek the inbreaking of your Spirit
to see what you see
and to live in ways that move us toward that vision . . .

God of enough, we thank you
that you give us access to every good thing
and empower us to be your people in this world.
Help us to live and act and pray according to our faith
in every part of our lives. **Amen.**

INVITATION TO OFFERING

The invitation to offering may be led from the Communion table.

Our world seeks to trap us in a mind-set of not-enough.
And yet everywhere we turn in Scripture
we know that this is not true.
One way in which we can disrupt the worldview of scarcity
is by giving freely and generously,
trusting and acting in ways that affirm our commitments.

You are invited to participate in this disruptive work
by the giving of your financial offerings.

INVITATION TO THE TABLE

The invitation to the table is led from the Communion table.

At this table we remember
that the feasting of God's people
is unbounded by time, space, or resources.
At this table there is always enough—
enough to nourish our spirits,
enough to feed our imaginations,
enough to keep us going even when it seems impossible.
At this table we remember
the story of God's abundance across the ages.

And so we gather with gratitude.

CHARGE

The blessing and charge may be led from the doors of the church.

Go forth from this place
knowing that there is enough,
trusting that there is enough,
and believing that God's abundance is available
in every place and at every time.
Amen. *or* **Thanks be to God.**

Proper 14

August 7–13

SEMICONTINUOUS READINGS

Genesis 37:1–4, 12–28   Romans 10:5–15
Psalm 105:1–6, 16–22, 45b   Matthew 14:22–33

OPENING SENTENCES

O give thanks to the Lord
and call on God's name.
**Proclaim the deeds of the Lord
to all the peoples.**

Sing to the Lord, sing praises to God.
Tell of all God's wonderful works.

Glory in God's holy name;
**seek the presence of the Lord,
rejoicing with all your heart.**

PRAYER OF THE DAY

O God, you have claimed us
as your beloved children,
clothing us with your grace.
Give us dreams and visions
of the coming of your holy realm,
where all are reconciled
to live in peace and safety;
through Jesus Christ our Lord. **Amen.**

*And how are they to proclaim him unless they are sent?
As it is written, "How beautiful are the feet of those who
bring good news!"*

Romans 10:15

INVITATION TO DISCIPLESHIP

The invitation to discipleship may be led from the baptismal font.

The Scriptures tell us,
"How beautiful are the feet of those
who bring good news!"

You are invited to discipleship—
to join in the beautiful journey
of proclaiming the good news
of Jesus Christ our Lord.
The path begins here and now.

PRAYERS OF INTERCESSION

The prayers of intercession may be led from the midst of the congregation.

The word of God is near to us,
on our lips and in our hearts.
Therefore we approach God in faith, saying:
Save us, O Lord; **hear our prayer.**

We pray for families divided by conflict.
Help us to seek reconciliation where possible,
and to protect those who are most vulnerable.
Save us, O Lord; **hear our prayer.**

We pray for victims of human trafficking.
Set free those who are held captive,
and deliver those who are in danger.
Save us, O Lord; **hear our prayer.**

We pray for those who cannot believe.
Let us be messengers of your good news
and witnesses to your saving work.
Save us, O Lord; **hear our prayer.**

We pray for those taking first steps in faith.
Guide their feet, calm their hearts,
and sustain them with your Spirit.
Save us, O Lord; **hear our prayer.**

Help us, O Lord,
to trust in your life-giving power—
to confess it with our lips
and believe it in our hearts—
that we may call on your name
and receive our salvation;
through Jesus Christ our Savior. **Amen.**

INVITATION TO OFFERING

The invitation to offering may be led from the Communion table.

The same Lord who protected Joseph
and delivered the people from famine
sets us free from every evil
and provides for our daily needs.

With gratitude for God's saving work,
let us offer our lives and gifts to the Lord.

INVITATION TO THE TABLE

The invitation to the table is led from the Communion table.

The Lord lifts us out of the pit
and gives us a place of honor
at the heavenly banquet—
where all are beloved children
and there is grace in abundance.

Come and join this holy feast.
Christ has prepared a place for you.

CHARGE

The blessing and charge may be led from the doors of the church.

Call on the name of the Lord,
and go forth to bring good news to others.
Amen. *or* **Thanks be to God.**

Proper 14

August 7–13

COMPLEMENTARY READINGS

1 Kings 19:9–18   Romans 10:5–15
Psalm 85:8–13   Matthew 14:22–33

OPENING SENTENCES

> Surely God's salvation is at hand.
> **Draw near to God**
> **and God will draw near to you.**
>
> Come, let us hear what God will speak,
> **for God will speak peace to God's people,**
> **to those who turn to God in their hearts.**

PRAYER OF THE DAY

> O God with us,
> your word is near,
> on our lips and in our hearts.
> In this moment,
> you come to us not as fire, storm, or quaking ground,
> but as the intimacy of our very breath,
> the sound of sheer silence.
> Be present in our places of fear,
> speak stillness to our trembling hearts,
> minister to us with bread and water and rest.
> Then send us from that rest
> to be present with all who long
> for the beautiful promise of your good news
> and the serenity of your steadfast love;
> through Jesus Christ our Lord. **Amen.**

INVITATION TO DISCIPLESHIP

The invitation to discipleship may be led from the baptismal font.

> O weary souls with seedling faith,
> we have been invited to rest and to trust.
>
> Will you, like Jesus, find space in your life
> to pray before the storm comes?
> Will you, like the disciples,
> learn to trust the one who draws near to you,
> or, like Elijah, to entrust your ministry to others?

PRAYERS OF INTERCESSION

The prayers of intercession may be led from the midst of the congregation.

> God of sheer silence and spoken peace,
> in the psalms you give us a glimpse
> of a world in which steadfast love and faithfulness meet
> and righteousness and peace kiss each other,
> in which all is made right
> because you have responded to those who turn to you.
>
> Though we do not yet live in that world,
> we come before you now,
> knowing that you desire to listen to us
> and to walk alongside us,
> as we hold close those who are longing
> for an experience of your presence.
>
> We hold close those who fear—
> for their churches,
> for their neighborhoods,
> for their country,
> for their lives,
> for their future,
> for their children.
> O God,
> your steadfast love drives out all fear.
> God of steadfast love, **draw near.**

We hold close those who grow weary—
of injustice,
of being overworked,
of being ignored,
of constant conflict,
of apathy,
of broken systems.
O God,
your faithfulness does not faint or grow weary.
God of faithfulness, **draw near.**

We hold close those who hunger—
for food,
for shelter,
for justice,
for renewal,
for rest,
for change.
O God,
in your righteousness there is life and abundance.
God of righteousness, **draw near.**

We hold close those who feel alone—
in their families,
in their communities,
in their pursuit of what is right,
in their suffering,
in their illness,
in their grief.
O God,
you call those who make peace your children,
and you will not forsake them.
God of peace, **draw near.**

As we hold close those who fear and grow weary,
who hunger and feel alone,
hold us close, O God.
Sustain us,
and make us your hands and feet
through the power of your Holy Spirit,
who prays with and through us. **Amen.**

INVITATION TO OFFERING

The invitation to offering may be led from the Communion table.

Our God gives to us what is good.

Let us in turn
give generously as we are able,
that we might share God's good gifts
and proclaim good news.

INVITATION TO THE TABLE

The invitation to the table is led from the Communion table.

The word is indeed near us,
on our lips and in our hearts.
As we partake together of this bread and cup,
as they pass through our lips,
may our hearts be changed.

All are welcome,
for God is generous to those
who call on the name of the Lord.
Come, taste and see that God is good.

CHARGE

The blessing and charge may be led from the doors of the church.

Go out, with beautiful feet,
to proclaim the good news
of a God who draws near
and says, "Take heart;
do not be afraid."
Amen. *or* **Thanks be to God.**

Proper 15

August 14–20

SEMICONTINUOUS READINGS

Genesis 45:1–15   Romans 11:1–2a, 29–32
Psalm 133   Matthew 15:(10–20) 21–28

OPENING SENTENCES

How good and pleasant it is
when the people of God live in unity!
**It is like being anointed with precious oil,
running down the head.**

It is like the morning dew,
falling upon the mountains of Zion.
**For there the Lord ordained this blessing:
life forevermore.**

PRAYER OF THE DAY

Holy God, by your providence
you have preserved your people
through many times of trouble.
Bless and keep us in these days,
that we may know your abundant love
and proclaim your saving work;
through Jesus Christ our Lord. **Amen.**

INVITATION TO DISCIPLESHIP

The invitation to discipleship may be led from the baptismal font.

This is the promise of the gospel:
God already knows you.
God already loves you.
God has already gifted you.
God has already called you.

You are invited—
to deepen this knowledge,
to feast in this love,
to cultivate these gifts,
and to follow this calling.

There is a place for you
among the people of God
in this community of faith.

PRAYERS OF INTERCESSION

The prayers of intercession may be led from the midst of the congregation.

With the boldness of faith
we come to God in prayer, saying:
Lord, help us; **hear our prayer**.

We pray for the leaders of nations.
Teach them to provide for the well-being
of all the people in their care.
Lord, help us; **hear our prayer.**

We pray for those who feel rejected.
Help them to know and trust
that your love will never forsake them.
Lord, help us; **hear our prayer.**

We pray for those who are oppressed.
Deliver them from their torment,
and give them lives of dignity and peace.
Lord, help us; **hear our prayer.**

We pray for those who are hungry.
Welcome them as beloved children,
and feed them with your abundant grace.
Lord, help us; **hear our prayer.**

O Lord our God, give us the faith
to put our prayers into practice
for the sake of this world you love
and for all those who are in need;
through Jesus Christ our Savior. **Amen.**

INVITATION TO OFFERING

The invitation to offering may be led from the Communion table.

God calls us to be good stewards
of the gifts of the earth
so there will be enough for everyone.

Let us share what we have,
entrusting the gifts of our lives
to the work of the Lord.

INVITATION TO THE TABLE

The invitation to the table is led from the Communion table.

Even in times of famine
God provides a table for us,
feeding us with mercy.

Come to this table—
where strangers become siblings
and foes become friends;
where wanderers are welcome
and humble ones are honored;
where the sick find salvation
and the outcast find open arms.

CHARGE

The blessing and charge may be led from the doors of the church.

Go forth to seek the Lord in faith
and you will be a blessing in the world.
Amen. *or* **Thanks be to God.**

Proper 15

August 14–20

COMPLEMENTARY READINGS

Isaiah 56:1, 6–8
Psalm 67

Romans 11:1–2a, 29–32
Matthew 15:(10–20) 21–28

OPENING SENTENCES

Let the peoples praise you, O God;
let all the peoples praise you.

Let the nations be glad and sing for joy,
**for you judge the peoples with equity
and guide the nations upon earth.**

Let the peoples praise you, O God;
let all the peoples praise you.

PRAYER OF THE DAY

God of all creatures and all people—
near and far,
outcast and insider,
rejected and embraced—
you continue to surpass our expectations
through your boundless love and faithfulness.
Grant us the humility to recognize
the ways you already move
among those who are strange to us,
and the empathy and courage
both to be strangely radical in our welcome
and to be received as strangers
among those you call us to love.
We pray this through the Holy Spirit,
our counselor and comforter,
who moves wild and windlike among us. **Amen.**

INVITATION TO DISCIPLESHIP

The invitation to discipleship may be led from the baptismal font.

Friends and strangers, our God gathers all.

Will we be willing to make this community
a house of prayer for all peoples?
Are we prepared for the joys and struggles,
the mistakes and the mercy
that it will take to become this house of prayer?

PRAYERS OF INTERCESSION

The prayers of intercession may be led from the midst of the congregation.

O gathering God,
as you shape us into a house of prayer for all peoples,
so shape our prayers
that the landscape of our empathy
might grow wider and wider.

We pray for those in this spiritual community
who are strangers to us.
They may sit in the pew next to us,
but we have not engaged with them,
and we do not know them.
They may be members
but never come to worship,
and we do not know them.
They may have ties to this community
but now live far away,
and we do not know them.
You know them, O God,
and you know their struggles and joys.
Make them known to us.

We pray for those in our neighborhood
who are strangers to us.
They may have once been part of this community
but are no longer,
and we do not know them.
They may live right next door
but have never stepped foot in this building,
and we do not know them.

They may live in fear of us, or in ignorance,
in hurt from something that happened here,
or oblivious that anything happens here,
and we do not know them.
You know them, O God,
and you know their struggles and joys.
Make them known to us.

We pray for those in this town
who are strangers to us.
They may be a part of another spiritual community,
or of none at all,
and we do not know them.
They may have access to wealth and privilege and power,
or they may not,
and we do not know them.
They may be the shapers of the systems in which we live,
or participants,
or they may be ground down by those same systems,
and we do not know them.
You know them, O God,
and you know their struggles and joys.
Make them known to us.

We pray for those in this country
who are strangers to us.
They may believe and make decisions
in ways that are strange to us,
or in ways that feel harmful to us,
and we do not know them.
They may have been born on this soil,
or brought here without their consent,
or risked everything to come here,
and we do not know them.
They may live in places or live in ways
that seem far away from all we have experienced,
and we do not know them.
You know them, O God,
and you know their struggles and joys.
Make them known to us.

O God, we pray for those on this continent
who are strangers to us.
They may share a border with us,
or they may be countries away,
and we do not know them.
They may speak a different language than we do,
or have a different political system,
or engage in cultural practices distinct from our own,
and we do not know them.
They may oppose us or agree with us,
chafe under the impact of our laws and actions,
or aspire to partner with us,
and we do not know them.
You know them, O God,
and you know their struggles and joys.
Make them known to us.

We pray for those in this world
who are strangers to us.
They may be at war with us,
or be partners in peace,
and we do not know them.
They may make the things that make our lives good,
or resent us for taking their goods,
and we do not know them.
They may be connected to us
through those who have come seeking new life here,
or through those we have sent to live among them,
and we do not know them.
You know them, O God,
and you know their struggles and joys.
Make them known to us.

O God, your love knows no bounds.
As you shape us into a house of prayer for all peoples,
so shape our actions
that they might embody our prayers.
May our love be as boundless as yours.
This we pray, through your wild, windlike Spirit. **Amen.**

INVITATION TO OFFERING

The invitation to offering may be led from the Communion table.

Come, let us join ourselves to our God
and to God's ministry to all in this world
through giving of ourselves and our resources.

INVITATION TO THE TABLE

The invitation to the table is led from the Communion table.

The earth has yielded its increase;
God, our God, has blessed us.

This table is God's table,
spread for all, and all are welcome.

CHARGE

The blessing and charge may be led from the doors of the church.

Live as those beloved by God,
who once were estranged
but now are part of God's household.
Live as if everyone you meet,
and those you will never meet,
are as beloved
and as at home with God
as you are.
Amen. *or* **Thanks be to God.**

Proper 16

August 21–27

SEMICONTINUOUS READINGS

Exodus 1:8–2:10   Romans 12:1–8
Psalm 124   Matthew 16:13–20

OPENING SENTENCES

If the Lord had not been with us,
**our enemies would have destroyed us
and the floods would have swept us away.**

Blessed be the Lord,
who has not forsaken us.

Our help is in the name of the Lord,
maker of heaven and earth.

PRAYER OF THE DAY

Holy God, through baptism
you save us from sin and evil
and deliver us from death.
Nourish us at your table
and train us for your service,
that we may help to set others free;
through Jesus Christ our Lord. **Amen.**

*[Jesus] said to them, "But who do you say that I am?" Simon Peter
answered, "You are the Messiah, the Son of the living God."*

Matthew 16:15–16

INVITATION TO DISCIPLESHIP

The invitation to discipleship may be led from the baptismal font.

The people of God are called
not to be conformed to this world,
but to be transformed—
by seeking the will of God
for our lives and for the world.
Through our common life and witness,
God is working to transform the world.

Will you join us in this calling?
Will you come and be transformed?

PRAYERS OF INTERCESSION

The prayers of intercession may be led from the midst of the congregation.

Let us open our hearts in prayer
to the Lord, the maker of heaven and earth, saying:
God, be with us; **hear our prayer.**

We pray for children who are in trouble.
Keep them safe from those who would harm them,
and deliver those who are neglected or abused.
God, be with us; **hear our prayer.**

We pray for nations plagued by warfare.
Take away the weapons of violence,
and make us instruments of peace.
God, be with us; **hear our prayer.**

We pray for those who serve others.
Give energy and encouragement
to all teachers, leaders, givers, and helpers.
God, be with us; **hear our prayer.**

We pray for people who are in prison.
Set us free from every kind of captivity—
addiction and affluence, poverty and prejudice.
God, be with us; **hear our prayer.**

Blessed are you, O Lord, for you have promised
to build us up as your church, the body of Christ.
Empower us to bind up all that is broken
and to set free those who are oppressed,
that the gates to your holy realm may be opened;
through Jesus Christ our Savior. **Amen.**

INVITATION TO OFFERING

The invitation to offering may be led from the Communion table.

We all have different gifts,
but we are members of one body.
We are called to present ourselves
as a living offering,
holy and acceptable to God.
This is our spiritual worship.

Let us offer our lives and our gifts
to God, the giver of life.

INVITATION TO THE TABLE

The invitation to the table is led from the Communion table.

We who are many are one body in Christ,
and individually we are members of one another.
When we gather at the Lord's table
we are united with God and one another
as members of the one body of Christ.

You are invited to share in this feast.
Come. Christ prepares a place for you here.

CHARGE

The blessing and charge may be led from the doors of the church.

Now go forth in faith to share your gifts,
seeking the will of God in the world.
Amen. *or* **Thanks be to God.**

Proper 16

August 21–27

COMPLEMENTARY READINGS

Isaiah 51:1–6   Romans 12:1–8
Psalm 138   Matthew 16:13–20

OPENING SENTENCES

We give thanks to you, O God, with our whole heart,
for your steadfast love and faithfulness.

On the day I called, you answered;
you increased my strength of soul.

All the rulers of earth shall praise you, O God.
We join them in singing of your ways,
for great is your glory.

PRAYER OF THE DAY

O Cornerstone,
though once you were rejected,
you have never rejected us
but have raised up for us a secure foundation
made of all the faithful who have come before
and those who surround us even now.
Fashion us, O God,
into a solid rock for others,
hewn from the saints who pursued your righteousness,
who sought you in the wilderness,
and who followed, though none came with them.
This we pray through Jesus Christ,
the master artisan and our sure foundation. **Amen.**

INVITATION TO DISCIPLESHIP

The invitation to discipleship may be led from the baptismal font.

Look to those who came before you,
to the quarry from which you were dug.
God calls us to follow their example,
to serve as rocks on which others might depend.

How might God be calling you
to share your journey with others,
to serve as part of their firm foundation
even when you feel like a stone rejected
or a wilderness place?

PRAYERS OF INTERCESSION

The prayers of intercession may be led from the midst of the congregation.

God, our refuge and our strength,
though we walk in the midst of trouble,
you stretch out your hand to deliver us.
Hear us now, as we bring our prayers to you.

Regard the lowly—
who look to the heavens for help;
who rise, though others keep a boot on their necks;
who carry your image, though some may not see it;
who daily encounter rejection of various kinds.
May they find your purpose for them fulfilled,
even as they know that you are near to them.
Your steadfast love, O God, endures forever.
Do not forsake the work of your hands.

Comfort those in waste places—
who feel that their lives are falling apart;
who think they have squandered their last good chance;
who see only ruin and rubble around them
as a consequence of their choices or the actions of others.
May they know joy and gladness in abundance
as you rebuild from the wreckage of their circumstance.
Your steadfast love, O God, endures forever.
Do not forsake the work of your hands.

Guide those in the wilderness—
who feel lost about where to go next;
who face daily anxiety and fear;
who wander in their grief;
whose journey has been plagued by illness or hardship.
May they emerge into an Eden
full of thanksgiving and the voice of song.
Your steadfast love, O God, endures forever.
Do not forsake the work of your hands.

Provide for those in the desert—
who hunger and thirst,
who long for shelter,
who pine for righteousness,
who seek your justice.
May they light upon a garden in which to dwell,
a place brimming with your goodness.
Your steadfast love, O God, endures forever.
Do not forsake the work of your hands.

On the day we called, O God, you answered.
Increase our strength of soul,
that even as we pray these prayers
you might shape us into a living temple
of your steadfast love and faithfulness
to those who long for a place of refuge.
Through Jesus Christ we pray. **Amen.**

INVITATION TO OFFERING

The invitation to offering may be led from the Communion table.

Siblings, by the mercies of our God,
let us present our whole selves
and all of our gifts
as living sacrifices, holy and acceptable,
so that we might discern God's will
and participate in God's work.

INVITATION TO THE TABLE

The invitation to the table is led from the Communion table.

We who are many are one in Christ.

As we come together to this table
to partake in this meal of bread and cup,
let us listen to God's voice
and look to what God has already done,
even as we anticipate how God will rebuild and remake us.

CHARGE

The blessing and charge may be led from the doors of the church.

Do not fear the wilderness
and the waste of rejection and ruin.
God is with you.
Look to those God has provided to you
as solid rocks and sure foundations,
even as God shapes you
into a stone of support for someone else.
Amen. *or* **Thanks be to God.**

Proper 17

August 28–September 3

SEMICONTINUOUS READINGS

Exodus 3:1–15   Romans 12:9–21
Psalm 105:1–6, 23–26, 45b   Matthew 16:21–28

OPENING SENTENCES

> The Lord our God is with us.
> **Stop and listen; turn and see!**
>
> The Lord our God is with us.
> **This place is holy ground.**
>
> The Lord our God is with us.
> **The God of our ancestors is here.**

PRAYER OF THE DAY

> Holy God, we give you thanks
> that you have spoken to us
> and revealed yourself to us
> through the gift of your word.
> Help us to heed your voice,
> that we may follow you faithfully
> and honor your glorious name;
> through Jesus Christ our Lord. **Amen.**

> *God said to Moses, "I AM WHO I AM." [God]*
> *said further, "Thus you shall say to the Israelites,*
> *'I AM has sent me to you.'"*
>
> *Exodus 3:14*

INVITATION TO DISCIPLESHIP

The invitation to discipleship may be led from the baptismal font.

Jesus said,
"If any want to become my followers,
let them deny themselves
and take up their cross and follow me."
Jesus promises that
those who seek to save their lives
will lose them,
but those who offer their lives freely
for the sake of the gospel
will find abundant life.

Are you ready to find abundant life?
Come and share in our calling
as disciples of the Lord Jesus Christ.

PRAYERS OF INTERCESSION

The prayers of intercession may be led from the midst of the congregation.

Through the practice of prayer,
we offer our lives in God's service, saying:
O Lord our God, **hear our prayer.**

We pray for those who question their calling.
Give courage, wisdom, and strength
to those whom you have called to serve you.
O Lord our God, **hear our prayer.**

We pray for those who are in captivity.
Show them a vision of your promised land,
and lead them out to worship you in freedom.
O Lord our God, **hear our prayer.**

We pray for those who struggle in faith.
Fill them with love, hope, and joy,
and help them live in harmony with all.
O Lord our God, **hear our prayer.**

We pray for those who are persecuted.
Let them glimpse your coming realm,
where there is justice for all people.
O Lord our God, **hear our prayer.**

Holy One, by the power of your Spirit
equip us to serve you faithfully
even through suffering and strife,
that we may share in your glory
at the coming of your new creation;
through Jesus Christ our Savior. **Amen.**

INVITATION TO OFFERING

The invitation to offering may be led from the Communion table.

We are called to rejoice in hope,
be patient in suffering, persevere in prayer,
and contribute to the needs of the saints.

With glad and generous hearts,
let us share the offerings of our life
with the Lord of all life.

INVITATION TO THE TABLE

The invitation to the table is led from the Communion table.

The Lord our God, the great I AM,
is with us in this place.
**Let us stop and stay here,
to share the table of our Lord.**

The God of our past,
present, and future
has prepared a feast for us.
**Let us stop and stay here,
to share the table of our Lord.**

CHARGE

The blessing and charge may be led from the doors of the church.

We have been set free for service.
Let us take up the cross and follow Jesus.
Amen. *or* **Thanks be to God.**

Proper 17

August 28—September 3

COMPLEMENTARY READINGS

Jeremiah 15:15–21

Psalm 26:1–8

Romans 12:9–21

Matthew 16:21–28

OPENING SENTENCES

O God, I love the house in which you dwell
and the place where your glory abides.

For your steadfast love is before my eyes,
and I walk in faithfulness to you.

Let us sing aloud a song of thanksgiving
and tell of all God's wondrous deeds.

PRAYER OF THE DAY

O Christ, who calls us to discipleship
through your life, death, and resurrection,
you made known to us the full cost
of living as your followers.
Though many of us still face violence and death
from those who are threatened by our trust in you,
many more encounter the mundane, but no less real, suffering
that comes through daily discipleship—
as we bless our persecutors,
associate with those brought low,
refrain from revenge,
and seek to live in peace.
Others find it difficult to accept the cost,
either because they have so much to lose,
or because other people have already taken so much from them.
Teach us how to lose our life
without treating ourselves as worthless.
Show us the way to find life
without exhausting ourselves
in trying to fashion our own salvation.

Demonstrate anew how it is
that you are the way, and the truth, and the life,
that we might find joy and delight in you.
In your name we pray. **Amen.**

INVITATION TO DISCIPLESHIP

The invitation to discipleship may be led from the baptismal font.

Just as he called his disciples,
so Jesus calls us to take up our cross and follow.

Will you take the time to discern
what is precious from what is worthless?
Will you do so in a way
that embodies mutual affection for others
and honors the image of God within you?

PRAYERS OF INTERCESSION

The prayers of intercession may be led from the midst of the congregation.

*In the Prayers of Intercession, the language of "the presence of justice" comes
from Martin Luther King Jr.,* Strive toward Freedom, *1958; the language
of "an environment where all can flourish" comes from Nelson Mandela,*
Message from Mr N. R. Mandela for the Global Convention on Peace
and Nonviolence in New Delhi, *2004.*

O God of healing, cross, and resurrection,
we rejoice in hope,
even as we wait for the end of suffering
and persevere in our prayers.
Pray with us now; incline your ear,
as we bring our lives before you.

As we try to bless those who persecute us,
make us aware of others facing persecution
and of the ways in which we persecute others.
May the suffering that emerges from one harassing others
come to a swift and certain end.
Lord, in your mercy, **hear our prayer.**

As we rejoice with those who rejoice
and weep with those who weep,
make us present to the full humanity
of those we walk alongside.
May those who live the complex reality
of joy mixed with sorrow
not be pushed to claim one or the other,
but may we all discover how to embody our full emotions,
while remaining open and receptive to the emotions of others.
Lord, in your mercy, **hear our prayer.**

As we attempt to live in harmony with one another,
make us mindful of those too often neglected
in attempts to balance the scales,
or those who are asked to bear the greater burden
of that balance.
May the wisdom of those less heard
be woven into the fabric of our communities,
even as those of us who get more attention
discern the wisdom of humility and listening.
Lord, in your mercy, **hear our prayer.**

As we refrain from repaying anyone evil for evil,
make us conscious of the root causes of evil in our world.
May we work together not only to treat the symptoms of evil,
but also to address the conditions that make evil possible.
Lord, in your mercy, **hear our prayer.**

As we seek to live peaceably with all,
make us alive to the full possibilities of peace,
not just the absence of conflict
but the presence of justice,
and an environment where all can flourish.
May we look for all the ways
that your peaceable kin-dom is already at work in our world.
Lord, in your mercy, **hear our prayer.**

O God, we lift up to you
our prayers for situations both near to us and far away,
knowing that you hear us
and call us to find ways to respond . . .

Worshipers may offer other prayers aloud or in silence.

All these things we pray in Jesus' name.
Lord, in your mercy, **hear our prayer. Amen.**

INVITATION TO OFFERING

The invitation to offering may be led from the Communion table.

Jesus comes to us with a provocative question:
"What will it profit you to gain the whole world,
but forfeit your life?
Or what will you give in return for your life?"

As we discern what we are being asked to give
in response to the life God has given us,
let us come before God not out of duty,
but with joy, delight, and thanks.

INVITATION TO THE TABLE

The invitation to the table is led from the Communion table.

We have tasted God's word
and been invited into joy and delight.

Let us continue the feast as we approach this table of grace,
where we remember Christ's life, death, and resurrection,
even as we wait for his return.

CHARGE

The blessing and charge may be led from the doors of the church.

Let your love be genuine,
hate what is evil,
hold fast to what is good,
seek what is precious,
take delight in the life God has given,
even as you lose it in pursuit of God's calling.
Amen. *or* **Thanks be to God.**

Proper 18

September 4–10

SEMICONTINUOUS READINGS

Exodus 12:1–14   Romans 13:8–14
Psalm 149   Matthew 18:15–20

OPENING SENTENCES

> Praise the Lord!
> **Sing to the Lord a new song;**
> **sing praise among the faithful.**
>
> Let the people of God be glad;
> **let us rejoice, dance, and sing.**
>
> For the Lord rejoices in the people;
> **God gives glory to the humble of heart.**

PRAYER OF THE DAY

> Holy God, you prepare a table for us
> in the presence of our enemies—
> the great feast of our salvation.
> Nourish us always at your table,
> that we may feed others
> with the promise of your saving love;
> through Jesus Christ our Lord. **Amen.**

INVITATION TO DISCIPLESHIP

The invitation to discipleship may be led from the baptismal font.

> The night is over; the day is dawning.
> Now is the time to wake from our sleep.
> The time of salvation has come.
>
> Are you ready to step into the light
> of this new day?
> We are eager to accompany you
> on the path of discipleship.

PRAYERS OF INTERCESSION

The prayers of intercession may be led from the midst of the congregation.

Joining hearts and minds together,
we ask for help from the Lord, saying:
God of our salvation, **hear our prayer.**

We pray for immigrants and refugees.
Give them safe passage and sanctuary;
let them find welcome and hospitality.
God of our salvation, **hear our prayer.**

We pray for those who are sick.
Comfort them in their affliction;
heal them in your tender mercy.
God of our salvation, **hear our prayer.**

We pray for neighbors in need.
Help us to care for one another;
show us how to share your love.
God of our salvation, **hear our prayer.**

We pray for the unity of the church.
Teach us to confess and forgive;
make us a sign of your reconciling work.
God of our salvation, **hear our prayer.**

Holy One, we give you thanks
that the Lord Jesus is among us
whenever we gather in his name.
Help us to be his body in the world,
that your will may be done
on earth as it is in heaven;
through Jesus Christ our Savior. **Amen.**

INVITATION TO OFFERING

The invitation to offering may be led from the Communion table.

In the household of the Lord
we share the gifts we have received,
that all may know God's abundant grace.

With generosity and joy
let us offer our lives to the Lord.

INVITATION TO THE TABLE

The invitation to the table is led from the Communion table.

This is a day of remembrance for us,
a day to celebrate as a festival of the Lord.
For the Lord Jesus Christ has called us
to keep this feast in remembrance of him.

Come to the table of the Lord
and share this feast of freedom.

CHARGE

The blessing and charge may be led from the doors of the church.

This is the fulfillment of God's law:
to love your neighbor as yourself.
Amen. *or* **Thanks be to God.**

Proper 18

September 4–10

COMPLEMENTARY READINGS

Ezekiel 33:7–11
Psalm 119:33–40

Romans 13:8–14
Matthew 18:15–20

OPENING SENTENCES

We know what time it is.
It is time to wake from our sleep!

Salvation is nearer to us now than when we first believed.
The night is far gone, the day is near!

Where two or three are gathered in Jesus' name,
God is here among us.

Let us worship God together.

PRAYER OF THE DAY

O source of love,
we know what love is
because you loved us first.
As we seek to follow your way,
let us neither be so single-minded in our pursuit
of personal righteousness
that we neglect the journeys of others,
nor so obsessed with the speck in our neighbor's eye
that we fail to notice the log in our own.
Make us sentinels,
vigilant in seeking your love in our lives,
so that we might owe no one anything
except for that love.
Enable us to confront evil when we see it,
especially when we find it in ourselves.
Help us to turn toward you,
so that we might inspire others to turn around too.
Through Christ, in Christ,
and by the power of the Holy Spirit we pray. **Amen.**

INVITATION TO DISCIPLESHIP

The invitation to discipleship may be led from the baptismal font.

Beloved of God,
when someone is baptized
they are asked to reject evil
and to profess their faith in Jesus Christ.

How can we more fully live into these commitments,
not only to turn from evil and toward Christ ourselves,
but also to help others live in that same way?
Are we willing to confront wrongdoing when we see it?
Will we walk alongside those
who travel a path that leads to death
in order to help them find and choose life?

PRAYERS OF INTERCESSION

The prayers of intercession may be led from the midst of the congregation.

God of every hour,
we live in twilight times—
the night is far gone, the day is near
but not yet dawning.
Even as we hope in you,
we lament what we see in the world around us
and the many ways that human beings
continue to choose death instead of life.

God, we pray for this home you have given us
and for the other creatures who inhabit it alongside us.
As species disappear,
ecosystems deteriorate,
and the earth warms,
enable us to turn from our deadly ways
and toward life in you.

God, we pray for our death-obsessed society.
We have invented thousands of ways to hurt each other
and thousands of reasons to do so.
We claim to be obsessed with living,
but we are merely preoccupied with avoiding
the death that swirls all around us.

Teach us to count our days,
that we may gain a wise heart.
Satisfy us in the morning with your steadfast love,
so that we may rejoice and be glad all our days.

God, we pray for those caught up in deadly systems.
Show us how to love our neighbors
who lack access to timely and affordable health care,
who face mass incarceration and wrongful imprisonment,
who struggle to escape economic exploitation and poverty,
and who are subjected to daily racism and xenophobia.
Empower us, through your Holy Spirit,
to proclaim release to people who are held captive
and freedom to those who are oppressed.

God, as we await the dawn of your love,
may we find ways every day to live
and to share with others the fullness of life you promise.
Hear the cries of our voices
and the prayers we have not mentioned in this space.
Wake us up to your goodness;
through Jesus Christ, the light of the world, we pray. **Amen.**

INVITATION TO OFFERING

The invitation to offering may be led from the Communion table.

Paul encourages us to owe nothing to each other
except love, for love is a fulfilling of the law.

Let us give to God and to this community
out of what we have received from God,
in a spirit of gratitude and love.

INVITATION TO THE TABLE

The invitation to the table is led from the Communion table.

We gather at this table
to find God already among us,
calling us to turn from death to life.
At this table we remember
that Christ made this journey from death to life.
We are not alone;
the path has already been traveled
by one who loves us.

In gratitude, then, let us come.
All has been made ready.
All are welcome.

CHARGE

The blessing and charge may be led from the doors of the church.

As you go forth in God's service,
follow the Lord Jesus Christ,
our bright morning star,
who leads us from death into life.
Amen. *or* **Thanks be to God.**

Proper 19

September 11–17

SEMICONTINUOUS READINGS

Exodus 14:19–31   Romans 14:1–12
Psalm 114 *or*   Matthew 18:21–35
  Exodus 15:1b–11, 20–21

OPENING SENTENCES

Sing to the Lord,
who has triumphed gloriously.
The Lord is our strength and might;
God has become our salvation.

Sing to the Lord,
who has triumphed gloriously.
This is our God, whom we praise;
the Lord is God's name.

PRAYER OF THE DAY

God our liberator,
as you delivered your people
from the armies of the pharaoh,
set us free from all evil,
that we may have faith in you
and tell the story of your great work
to every coming generation.
Through Christ we pray. **Amen.**

*Why is it, O sea, that you flee? O Jordan, that you
turn back? . . . Tremble, O earth, at the presence
of the LORD, at the presence of the God of Jacob.*

Psalm 114:5–7

INVITATION TO DISCIPLESHIP

The invitation to discipleship may be led from the baptismal font.

In this community of faith
we welcome all disciples of Jesus:
those who are strong
and those who are weak,
those who are confident
and those who are doubting,
those who are observant
and those who are forgetful.

Whoever you are
and wherever you come from,
there is a place for you
among the people of God.

PRAYERS OF INTERCESSION

The prayers of intercession may be led from the midst of the congregation.

Life-giving, liberating God,
we entrust to you this day
all the concerns of our hearts
and all the troubles of the world.
Hear our prayers:

for those who are fleeing war and violence . . .

for people seeking freedom from oppression . . .

for the healing and restoration of the earth . . .

for loved ones who are sick or suffering . . .

for those at the beginning or end of life . . .

for people struggling with financial burdens . . .

for all who are seeking forgiveness . . .

Lead us from captivity to freedom,
from sin to salvation,
and from death to life eternal;
through Jesus Christ our Lord. **Amen.**

INVITATION TO OFFERING

The invitation to offering may be led from the Communion table.

We do not live to ourselves,
and we do not die to ourselves.
Whether we live or whether we die,
we belong to the Lord.

Trusting in the God of life,
who raised Jesus from the dead,
let us offer our whole lives to the Lord.

INVITATION TO THE TABLE

The invitation to the table is led from the Communion table.

At this table we give thanks
for all of God's goodness and grace.
At this table we remember
the dying and rising of Jesus Christ.
At this table we join in prayer
for the gifts of the Holy Spirit.
Let us give thanks.
Let us remember.
Let us pray.

CHARGE

The blessing and charge may be led from the doors of the church.

Let your whole life be a joyful song
to the God of our salvation.
Amen. *or* **Thanks be to God.**

Proper 19

September 11–17

COMPLEMENTARY READINGS

Genesis 50:15–21   Romans 14:1–12
Psalm 103:(1–7) 8–13   Matthew 18:21–35

OPENING SENTENCES

Bless the Lord, my soul.
Bless God's holy name.

God is merciful and gracious,
slow to anger
and abounding in steadfast love.
God's steadfast love
stretches from earth to the heavens.
It never ends.

PRAYER OF THE DAY

Merciful God,
we come together with full hearts,
knowing that your compassion for us
is from everlasting to everlasting.
The gifts you have given us
are too great to ever be repaid.
The love you have for us
is more than we can comprehend.
As we come before you this day in worship,
may we feel no fear but come with joy and praise,
bowing before you as children and servants,
filled with gratitude for your steadfast love. **Amen.**

INVITATION TO DISCIPLESHIP

The invitation to discipleship may be led from the baptismal font.

Peter asks how many times he must forgive
in order to find the limit.
Jesus' forgiveness is unlimited.
We cannot pretend to match
the grace and compassion of God,
but with Jesus' invitation we can seek to break
long-lasting chains of fury and resentment.

Bring to mind a debt or a judgment you wish to release.
Make a fist, and imagine it closed up tight in your hand.
Trusting in Christ's forgiveness,
lift up one finger of your balled-up fist
and picture a slow release of your anger.
As you go through the week,
continue opening your hand, one finger at a time,
finding your way to greater forgiveness and freedom.

PRAYERS OF INTERCESSION

The prayers of intercession may be led from the midst of the congregation.

The five-finger prayer, a concept taught by Pope Francis, can be a model for children and adults at church and at home. Invite worshipers to focus on or touch each finger as they pray. You may include other prayer concerns wherever they fit best.

God of all, the fingers of our hands
help us bring our prayer concerns to you.

Our thumb reminds us to pray for those
who are closest to us—our family and friends . . .
God, some of those people are sick;
we pray for their health and wholeness.
Some are filled with the joys
of new life, new jobs, new homes.
Some are struggling with challenges
at school or at work.
Others are finding success and fulfillment,
and we could not be more grateful.

Our pointer finger reminds us to pray for those
who help point us in the right direction . . .
God, for our teachers we give thanks
and ask for continued strength, joy, and patience.
For doctors and nurses and home caregivers
who guide us to better health,
may they remain healthy, hopeful, and attentive.
For pastors and mentors and coaches,
may they listen well and speak wisely.
For police officers and firefighters,
may their desire to protect and serve cover us all.

Our tallest finger reminds us to pray for those
in positions of power . . .
God, we ask that you help guide
the decisions and actions of our leaders.
Whether they be school board members,
leaders in state or national government,
or our supervisors at work,
we ask that your will be accomplished
through their thoughts and actions.

Our ring finger is our weakest finger;
it reminds us to pray for those in greatest need . . .
God, for all those who are in trouble or in pain,
we ask your protection, provision, healing, and strength.
For those who feel their choices are at an end,
who cannot find a way to escape their addiction,
who are forced to choose
between paying for food or rent or medicine,
stay close to them.
If we are among those in great need,
give us the strength and the hope to ask for help
and to allow others to see, listen, and respond
to the needs we express.

Our pinky finger reminds us
that we can also pray for ourselves . . .
God, we give thanks for all that brings us joy
and for the many gifts we have received.
We also hold concerns in our hearts that we entrust to you.
Whether those concerns are big or small,
we know that you will listen to all of our prayers.

O God, your steadfast love is from everlasting to everlasting.
With confidence, we offer all these prayers to you;
in Jesus' name. **Amen.**

INVITATION TO OFFERING

The invitation to offering may be led from the Communion table.

We do not live to ourselves.
We do not die to ourselves.
If we live, we live to the Lord,
and if we die, we die to the Lord.
So then, whether we live or whether we die,
we are the Lord's.

Everything we have and everything we are
is from God.
Let us return our gifts
of time, talent, and treasure
to God and God's people.

INVITATION TO THE TABLE

The invitation to the table is led from the Communion table.

This table is not one of judgment but of grace.
Forgiven, we are sent out to forgive others.
But we must have bread for that journey.
All are invited to come to the table of God—
to join with Christ and with those in every time and place,
and to be nourished, strengthened, and renewed.

Come—eat, drink, and be filled.

CHARGE

The blessing and charge may be led from the doors of the church.

May all that is in you bless God.
May we follow in Christ's footsteps
of mercy and compassion.

May the Holy Spirit guide you on your journey.
Forgiven, may we seek to forgive.
Amen. *or* **Thanks be to God.**

Proper 20

September 18–24

SEMICONTINUOUS READINGS

Exodus 16:2–15   Philippians 1:21–30
Psalm 105:1–6, 37–45   Matthew 20:1–16

OPENING SENTENCES

Remember the wonderful work of the Lord—
who brought us out of captivity,

who fed us with bread from heaven
and gave us water from a stone.

God will never forget the promise;
therefore let us rejoice and sing!

PRAYER OF THE DAY

God our provider,
as you fed your people in the wilderness
with meat in the evening
and manna in the morning,
let your grace be our daily bread,
that we might be nourished in faith
and grow as your holy people.
Through Christ we pray. **Amen.**

INVITATION TO DISCIPLESHIP

The invitation to discipleship may be led from the baptismal font.

We are called to live our lives
in a manner that is worthy
of the gospel of Jesus Christ.
But we can't do this on our own.
We rely on the gifts of the Spirit
and the support of this community,
striving side by side in faith.

Will you join us in this holy work?

PRAYERS OF INTERCESSION

The prayers of intercession may be led from the midst of the congregation.

Generous, gracious God,
we know that you love this world
and are always seeking our good.
Hear our prayers:

for all who are hungry . . .

for the right use of the earth's resources . . .

for nations and communities that are divided . . .

for those who are facing death . . .

for loved ones who are far away . . .

for people who are seeking work . . .

for equal opportunities and fair wages . . .

Continue to shower your mercy upon us,
that there may be peace and plenty for all.
Nourish us with your grace
and sustain us for the journey of faith,
that we may live as your holy people;
through Jesus Christ our Lord. **Amen.**

INVITATION TO OFFERING

The invitation to offering may be led from the Communion table.

God provides all that we need—
bread enough for each day.
Our calling is to be good stewards
of the generous gifts of God,
sharing out of our abundance
and caring for those in need.

Trusting in God's grace,
let us present our lives to the Lord.

INVITATION TO THE TABLE

The invitation to the table is led from the Communion table.

God prepares a table for us
with the bread of heaven:
the body of our Lord Jesus Christ,
a gift of grace for all.

Come, taste and see
the goodness of the Lord.

CHARGE

The blessing and charge may be led from the doors of the church.

We may depart from this place,
but Christ is always with us.
Let us live our lives in a way
that is worthy of the gospel,
bearing witness to Christ in the world.
Amen. *or* **Thanks be to God.**

Proper 20

September 18–24

COMPLEMENTARY READINGS

Jonah 3:10–4:11
Psalm 145:1–8

Philippians 1:21–30
Matthew 20:1–16

OPENING SENTENCES

> Today and every day
> let us praise God's name.
> **Great is the Lord**
> **and greatly to be praised.**
>
> Today we will think on your wondrous works.
> **Today we will proclaim your awesome deeds.**
>
> Let us join together to worship our God
> in word, prayer, and song.

Inspired by Jesus' image of the first being last, worship planners might consider a change to the order of worship: beginning with the blessing and charge and sending the congregation out with a call to worship. If these opening sentences become the charge, the last line could be "Having worshiped in word, prayer, and song, let us go out and continue our worship of God."

PRAYER OF THE DAY

> Gracious God, your love for us
> is both a blessing and a challenge.
> May we be so filled with your love
> that it stretches us in this time of worship,
> opening us to new lengths and depths
> and new ways of reflecting your love to others.
> Encourage our spirits by your Spirit
> as we turn to you in praise and prayer.
> Inspire us to proclaim your greatness
> in word and deed,
> now and in the days to come. **Amen.**

INVITATION TO DISCIPLESHIP

The invitation to discipleship may be led from the baptismal font.

Showing God's love can be hard.
When we are frustrated with others,
we are asked to practice a generosity of spirit
we don't always feel.

Who in your life might benefit this week
from an extra dose of compassion?
Where might you practice extravagance
without bothering to measure what is deserved?

PRAYERS OF INTERCESSION

The prayers of intercession may be led from the midst of the congregation.

God of abundance, looking out the window
we can see just a sliver of your creativity and generosity.
The variety of animals, plants, bugs, and people
we pass in one day is enormous.
We give you thanks for the glorious splendor all around us.

Some of us can enjoy that splendor
without worrying about the roof over our heads,
or where the next meal will come from,
or the safety of our family—
and for that we are grateful.
Help us to recognize and live out our abundance
by using the extra energy and resources we have
to improve the lives of others.

Some of us cannot focus on what is outside our window
because of the chaos inside our homes.
Whether it is anxiety about paying the bills,
uncertainty about whether tonight will bring flowers or bruises,
or unkind voices in our own heads,
we ask that your steadfast love will feel tangible to us
and that our suffering will cease.

Give us a sense, God, of your fairness.
Encourage us not to keep score but to seek good for all.
Open our hearts and our minds.
Open our wallets and our tightly clenched fists.
We know that you give not as the world gives,
so teach us, guide us, direct us, and inspire us
with your Spirit of generosity;
in Jesus' name we pray. **Amen.**

INVITATION TO OFFERING

The invitation to offering may be led from the Communion table.

God is more generous with us
than we have cause to expect.
May we expect of ourselves more generosity.

There are many ways we can return thanks to God
through our gifts.
Whether in word or in deed,
in gifts of money or time,
let us offer our best to God in gratitude.

INVITATION TO THE TABLE

The invitation to the table is led from the Communion table.

God's abundant grace came to the people of Nineveh.
God's abundant grace came to the workers in the vineyard.
God's abundant grace came to the church in Philippi,
and it continues to come to us today—here at this table.
Here, once again, we see God's abundant goodness.
Here, once again, we see God's steadfast love.

Friends, welcome to this table of grace.
Come and enjoy the feast.

CHARGE

The blessing and charge may be led from the doors of the church.

> Friends, go into the vineyard
> and seek the good of all,
> at all times of the day and week.
> Do not grumble, but be generous,
> in deed and in spirit.
> **Amen.** *or* **Thanks be to God.**

Inspired by Jesus' image of the last being first, worship planners might consider a change to the order of worship: beginning with the blessing and charge and sending the congregation out with a call to worship. If this charge becomes the opening sentences, the first line could be "Welcome, friends, you have come in from the vineyard to seek sustenance from the vine. As we worship, may you be refreshed and renewed."

Proper 21

September 25–October 1

SEMICONTINUOUS READINGS

Exodus 17:1–7
Psalm 78:1–4, 12–16

Philippians 2:1–13
Matthew 21:23–32

OPENING SENTENCES

We share the stories of our ancestors,
things we have heard and known—

how the Lord divided the sea
and let the peoples pass through;
**how God split open rocks
to give us drink in the desert.**

We will not hide these stories from our children;
**we will tell the coming generations
about the glorious deeds of the Lord.**

PRAYER OF THE DAY

God our sustainer,
as you broke open a stone
to provide water for your people,
open our hearts to your mercy
and fill us with spiritual gifts,
that we may overflow with praise
all the days of our lives.
Through Christ we pray. **Amen.**

*Let the same mind be in you that was in Christ Jesus, who,
though he was in the form of God, did not regard equality
with God as something to be exploited, but emptied himself.*

Philippians 2:5–7a

INVITATION TO DISCIPLESHIP

The invitation to discipleship may be led from the baptismal font.

We believe that God is at work in you,
empowering you with spiritual gifts
and equipping you for joyful service.
We want to help you identify those gifts
and discern how God is calling you.

You are invited to join
this community of disciples
as we seek the will of God for the world.

PRAYERS OF INTERCESSION

The prayers of intercession may be led from the midst of the congregation.

Saving, sustaining God,
we give thanks for your great compassion,
welling up and overflowing
for all who are in need.
Hear our prayers:

for all who are thirsty . . .

for clean rivers, lakes, and oceans . . .

for leaders seeking wisdom . . .

for people who are abused and exploited . . .

for those who live in fear . . .

for the repair of broken promises . . .

for neighbors we too often overlook . . .

Pour out the gifts of your Spirit
to satisfy our thirsty souls,
that we may know and trust
your presence among us;
through Jesus Christ our Lord. **Amen.**

INVITATION TO OFFERING

The invitation to offering may be led from the Communion table.

Since we share the mind of Christ Jesus,
let us look not to our own interests,
but to the interests of others.

Let us glorify the living God
with the offering of our lives.

INVITATION TO THE TABLE

The invitation to the table is led from the Communion table.

At the table of the Lord
we share in the one Spirit.
At the table of the Lord
we share in the body of Christ.
At the table of the Lord
we share in the glory of God.

Come to this table,
where our cups overflow with joy.

CHARGE

The blessing and charge may be led from the doors of the church.

The Lord is with us.
Let us go forth in love and service,
sharing the grace of God with all.
Amen. *or* **Thanks be to God.**

Proper 21

September 25–October 1

COMPLEMENTARY READINGS

Ezekiel 18:1–4, 25–32   Philippians 2:1–13
Psalm 25:1–9   Matthew 21:23–32

OPENING SENTENCES

God, we lift our souls to you.
Make us to know your ways,
and teach us your paths.

Lead us in your truth, O God,
for you are our salvation.
For you we wait, all day long.

PRAYER OF THE DAY

Good and gracious God,
we come to be instructed in your way,
to be encouraged in Christ,
to be consoled by love,
and to share in the joy of the Spirit.
Do your work within us, God,
as we gather to worship you.
Guide us in your will
and lead us in your way.
Open our hearts and minds
that we may recognize your call.
In Jesus' name we pray. **Amen.**

INVITATION TO DISCIPLESHIP

The invitation to discipleship may be led from the baptismal font.

Paul writes to the Philippians,
"Let the same mind be in you that was in Christ Jesus."
He extends the same call to us.
But how do we discern that mind?

How do we know what to do?
We cannot know without being in relationship,
without being in conversation with God.

Find five minutes in your day
to sit quietly with God and listen.
You might breathe in and out,
alternating between deep silence and prayer,
saying, "Let my mind *[inhale]*
be Christ's mind *[exhale]*."

PRAYERS OF INTERCESSION

The prayers of intercession may be led from the midst of the congregation.

*The breath prayer suggested for the invitation to discipleship may also
be practiced during these prayers of intercession, as indicated below. The
leader may use words or gestures to guide worshipers in their breathing.*

We are called to pray without ceasing,
to pray with every breath:
Let our minds *[inhale]*
be Christ's mind *[exhale]*.

Creator, Sustainer, and Redeemer,
to you, O God, we lift up our souls.
We trust you, and so we turn to you
and call upon your holy name.
Let our minds *[inhale]*
be Christ's mind *[exhale]*.

We give thanks for the wonder of your creation,
and we pray for your forgiveness
for the ways we have caused it harm.
We offer praise for the gifts of sky and sea,
plant and animal, vine and vineyard,
yet we know that we have failed
to be the stewards you have called us to be.
Change our minds, Lord,
so we might go and do your work.
Let our minds *[inhale]*
be Christ's mind *[exhale]*.

We give thanks for love and goodness
we have witnessed this week—
for moments of deep contentedness,
for the gift of truths told,
for rays of hope that poked through the clouds,
for the people who have shown us love and care.
We take a moment in silence
to give thanks for the joys we experienced this week . . .
Let our minds *[inhale]*
be Christ's mind *[exhale]*.

If we are honest, God, we cannot claim only joy.
We have carried burdens as well—
for violence happening in *[specific places may be named]*,
for the unfairness of *[specific situations may be named]*,
for fears sparked by *[specific issues may be named]*.
We take a moment in silence
to bring to you the concerns we have shouldered . . .
Let our minds *[inhale]*
be Christ's mind *[exhale]*.

We thank you for your church—
for this community
and for your people in all places—
that we can tend to one another,
instruct one another,
and rely on one another.
May we help one another discern your will
so that we may be your hands and feet in the world.
Let our minds *[inhale]*
be Christ's mind *[exhale]*.

Let our minds *[inhale]*
be Christ's mind *[exhale]*.

Let our minds *[inhale]*
be Christ's mind *[exhale]*. **Amen.**

INVITATION TO OFFERING

The invitation to offering may be led from the Communion table.

> We are invited to go into the vineyard and share our gifts.
> Those gifts may be financial gifts.
> Those gifts may be spiritual gifts.
> Whether large or small, they are gifts to God.
>
> Whatever they may be, may we offer them humbly,
> with deep gratitude for all God has done for us.

INVITATION TO THE TABLE

The invitation to the table is led from the Communion table.

> Friends, this table is God's table.
> It is not a table of finery and excess,
> though it is a fine and abundant table.
>
> Friends, this table is God's table.
> It is not a table of "mine" or of "yours";
> it does not conform to the values of this world.
>
> This is a table where there are no enemies.
> This is a table where sinners are welcome.
> This is a table where you may find
> as many questions as answers.
> This is a table where Jesus is host,
> as both servant and Lord.
>
> This is God's table, friends,
> and you are all welcome.

CHARGE

The blessing and charge may be led from the doors of the church.

> Hear this charge from Paul:
> "Do nothing from selfish ambition or conceit,
> but in humility regard others as better than yourselves.
> Let each of you look not to your own interests,
> but to the interests of others.
> Let the same mind be in you that was in Christ Jesus."
> **Amen.** *or* **Thanks be to God.**

Proper 22

October 2–8

SEMICONTINUOUS READINGS

Exodus 20:1–4, 7–9, 12–20
Psalm 19

Philippians 3:4b–14
Matthew 21:33–46

OPENING SENTENCES

> The law of the Lord is perfect,
> reviving the soul;
> **the decrees of the Lord are sure,**
> **making wise the simple.**
>
> Let the words of our mouths
> and the meditations of our hearts
> be acceptable to the Lord,
> **for God is our rock and redeemer.**

PRAYER OF THE DAY

> God our deliverer,
> as you revealed your law
> to Moses at Mount Sinai,
> teach us to worship you alone
> and to keep your commandments,
> that we live by our faith
> and be faithful as your people.
> Through Christ we pray. **Amen.**

INVITATION TO DISCIPLESHIP

The invitation to discipleship may be led from the baptismal font.

> If you want to know Christ—
> the depth of his suffering and death
> and the power of his resurrection—
> we invite you to join us
> in this beloved community of faith.
>
> Let us press on together toward the goal
> for the prize of the heavenly call of God in Christ Jesus.

PRAYERS OF INTERCESSION

The prayers of intercession may be led from the midst of the congregation.

Creative, covenant-making God,
we come to you in faith,
seeking your way in the world
and your will for our lives.
Hear our prayers:

for the wisdom to know what is right . . .

for the courage to speak the truth . . .

for the strength to resist temptation . . .

for your mercy when we fail . . .

for people who are persecuted . . .

for loved ones who have suffered loss . . .

for the coming of your promised realm . . .

Continue to speak your word to us.
Let it shape our lives for your service,
that we may follow you faithfully
and be the people you have called us to be;
through Jesus Christ our Lord. **Amen.**

INVITATION TO OFFERING

The invitation to offering may be led from the Communion table.

Whatever gains we might possess,
we regard these as loss
compared to the surpassing value
of knowing Jesus Christ our Lord.

With great thanksgiving
for the grace of Jesus Christ,
let us offer our lives to the Lord.

INVITATION TO THE TABLE

The invitation to the table is led from the Communion table.

The gifts of the Lord are good,
rejoicing the heart.
The grace of the Lord is abundant,
reviving the soul.
The love of the Lord is faithful,
enduring forever.

Christ has prepared a table for us.
Come and share this covenant meal.

CHARGE

The blessing and charge may be led from the doors of the church.

You have heard the commandments of God.
Go and let your life bear witness
to the saving word of the Lord.
Amen. *or* **Thanks be to God.**

Proper 22

October 2–8

COMPLEMENTARY READINGS

Isaiah 5:1–7
Psalm 80:7–15

Philippians 3:4b–14
Matthew 21:33–46

OPENING SENTENCES

> The stone that the builders rejected
> has become the cornerstone.
> **This was the Lord's doing,**
> **and it is amazing in our eyes.**
>
> May the word of God amaze us again today.

PRAYER OF THE DAY

> God of vines and vineyards,
> we are the fruit of your creation.
> Tend to us so we may grow.
> Water our roots.
> Prune our branches.
> Inspect the fruit we produce.
> Shine your light upon us.
> Make us your own.
> In Jesus' name we pray. **Amen.**

> *Jesus said to them, "Have you never read in the scriptures: 'The stone that the builders rejected has become the cornerstone; this was the Lord's doing, and it is amazing in our eyes'?"*
>
> *Matthew 21:42*

INVITATION TO DISCIPLESHIP

The invitation to discipleship may be led from the baptismal font.

Sometimes we do not choose the better way.
We have made our confession
and we are indeed forgiven,
but we must continue to be honest.
We all sin and fall short of the glory of God,
again and again.
We do not have to wait until Sunday
to offer our confessions.
We can go to God at any time
having done a fearless and searching moral inventory.

This week let us accept the invitation
to take responsibility for our failings each night
and to trust the gift of God's grace
as it strengthens us to make better choices for the next day.

PRAYERS OF INTERCESSION

The prayers of intercession may be led from the midst of the congregation.

Today in this house for all—
both sinners and saints—
we come to you, God,
to pray for your wisdom and your grace.
In Christ we are a new creation!

Open our hearts when they are small—
when we reject your call for justice,
fearing it will require too much of us.
Break open our stingy outlook,
and bring us into the rhythms of your abundance.
In Christ we are a new creation!

Open our hands when they are clenched too tightly—
when we sing the songs of nationalism
more than we do the hymns of your praise.
May we reach out to those who have left all they know,
afraid of where they have come from
and unsure of where they are going.
In Christ we are a new creation!

Open our eyes when we would rather keep them closed—
when we look away from our neighbor
instead of looking into ways we can be of help.
Sharpen our vision so that we may see them from far away
and search for clothes, shoes, and food to share.
In Christ we are a new creation!

Open our minds when they are shut—
blocked by the certainty of our own opinion
rather than exposed to your radical love and grace.
Help us to be agents of your reconciling peace,
regarding no one from our human point of view,
but with the mind of Christ.
In Christ we are a new creation!

With the strength, power, and joy
of the triune God we say: **Amen.**

INVITATION TO OFFERING

The invitation to offering may be led from the Communion table.

God brought a vine out of Egypt
and planted it.
God cleared the ground
so that the vine could take deep root.
God continues to bring us out of difficult places.
We are invited to bloom where we are planted.

Let us offer our time and talents and treasure
with thanksgiving for all God has done for us.
May our gifts be added to the gifts of God,
in gratitude and in service of the whole people of God.

INVITATION TO THE TABLE

The invitation to the table is led from the Communion table.

> The wine from God's vineyard is the wine of salvation.
> The bread from God's vineyard is the bread of life.
> The meal at this table is a meal of abundant grace.
>
> Come. Look. Taste.
> Christ has made the table ready,
> and each of you is his honored guest.

CHARGE

The blessing and charge may be led from the doors of the church.

> The power of the resurrection makes all things new.
> Go out, knowing that Christ has made you his own.
> Forget what lies behind,
> and strain forward to what lies ahead.
> Go with God.
> **Amen.** *or* **Thanks be to God.**

Proper 23

October 9–15

OPENING SENTENCES

> Praise the Lord!
> **Give thanks to the Lord, for God is good;**
> **God's steadfast love endures forever.**
>
> Remember us, O Lord,
> when you show favor to your people;
> **let us know the blessing of your chosen ones**
> **and the gladness of those you love.**

PRAYER OF THE DAY

> God our redeemer,
> as you showed mercy to your people
> when they worshiped a false idol,
> be gracious to us and forgive us
> when we fall into temptation,
> that we may repent and return
> to worship and serve you alone.
> Through Christ we pray. **Amen.**

They made a calf at Horeb and worshiped a cast image.
They exchanged the glory of God for the image of an ox
that eats grass. They forgot God, their Savior, who had
done great things in Egypt.

Psalm 106:19–21

INVITATION TO DISCIPLESHIP

The invitation to discipleship may be led from the baptismal font.

Euodia, Syntyche, Clement—
we may not know much
about these leaders in the church at Philippi,
but we know that they were colleagues with Paul,
struggling in the work of the gospel,
standing firm in the way of the Lord.
We are called to join their number,
to share with them the mind of Christ Jesus,
rejoicing always in the Lord.

Will you come and join them?
Will you let your name join their names
in the book of life?

PRAYERS OF INTERCESSION

The prayers of intercession may be led from the midst of the congregation.

Mighty, merciful God,
you encourage us not to worry
but to make our requests known to you,
trusting in your goodness.
Hear our prayers:

for those who worship false idols . . .

for those who seek security in status or wealth . . .

for the healing of earth from disaster . . .

for loved ones who are struggling . . .

for people who have no peace . . .

for those without homes or good clothing . . .

for the strength to pursue our calling . . .

Fill us with gentleness and joy,
give us the peace that passes understanding,
and guard our hearts and minds;
through Jesus Christ our Lord. **Amen.**

INVITATION TO OFFERING

The invitation to offering may be led from the Communion table.

The Lord desires steadfast love, not sacrifice,
the knowledge of God rather than burnt offerings.

Let us offer our gifts and lives to the Lord
by doing justice, showing mercy,
and walking humbly with our God.

INVITATION TO THE TABLE

The invitation to the table is led from the Communion table.

We are invited to a great banquet—
the wedding feast of a new creation
at the marriage of heaven and earth.
All who clothe themselves
with the righteousness and grace of Christ
are welcome at this table.

Come and rejoice in this holy meal.

CHARGE

The blessing and charge may be led from the doors of the church.

Keep on doing the things
that you have learned and received
and heard and seen
through Christ Jesus,
and the God of peace will be with you.
Amen. *or* **Thanks be to God.**

Proper 23

October 9–15

COMPLEMENTARY READINGS

Isaiah 25:1–9   Philippians 4:1–9
Psalm 23   Matthew 22:1–14

OPENING SENTENCES

Rejoice in the Lord always;
again I say, Rejoice!
**Do not worry about anything,
but in everything by prayer
and supplication with thanksgiving
let your requests be made known to God.**

Let us bring all that we are to God in worship.

PRAYER OF THE DAY

Lord, you are our shepherd;
we shall not want.
You make us lie down in green pastures
and lead us beside still waters.
You restore our souls
and lead us in right paths
for your name's sake.
Even though we walk
through the valley of the shadow of death,
we fear no evil, for you are with us;
your rod and your staff comfort us.
You prepare a table before us
in the presence of our enemies.
You anoint our heads with oil;
our cups overflow.
Surely goodness and mercy
shall follow us all the days of our lives,
and we shall dwell in your house, O Lord,
our whole life long. **Amen.**

INVITATION TO DISCIPLESHIP

The invitation to discipleship may be led from the baptismal font.

> You are invited to the wedding banquet.
> Will you come?
> What good gift will you offer?
> Will it be
> something honorable?
> Something just?
> Something pure, pleasing, commendable?
>
> How can you offer that gift this week?

PRAYERS OF INTERCESSION

The prayers of intercession may be led from the midst of the congregation.

> God, our shepherd,
> it is easy to want for more, or better, or extra.
> As you lay us down in your pasture,
> remind us that there is none greener.
> Still the waters that roil within us.
> May our souls feel restored as we turn to you.
> Help us accompany others on your right paths.
>
> God, there are many who are walking
> through dark or difficult valleys right now:
> those who have lost their jobs;
> those who have lost dear ones;
> those who are lost without a country,
> scared to go home but here without legal papers;
> those with chronic pain or illnesses,
> as well as those who take care of them;
> those who remain captive to addiction;
> those we name aloud or in silence . . .
>
> Show us how to reach out
> and hold hands on your path
> so that none of us need fear.
> For you are with us;
> your rod and your staff will always comfort us.

Let us sit at table with all your people
and count none of them as our enemies:
neither Jew nor Greek,
black nor white,
male nor female,
Democrat nor Republican,
gay nor straight,
old nor young,
nor any others
between or beyond those binaries.

Then surely our cups will overflow,
and goodness and mercy will follow us
all the days of our lives,
and we will dwell in your house, O Lord,
our whole lives long. **Amen.**

INVITATION TO OFFERING

The invitation to offering may be led from the Communion table.

In Philippians, Paul invites us
to make our requests known to God.
But we are also invited to offer our gifts to God.
Having been led by still waters,
cared for as we walked through the darkest valley,
anointed with oil,
with our cup overflowing,
it is our turn to turn to God in thanks.

Let us offer our gifts to God
with gratitude and praise.

INVITATION TO THE TABLE

The invitation to the table is led from the Communion table.

This banquet table is for everyone.
Each of you is invited.
The bread has been prepared.
The cup is ready.
It does not matter what you wear to this feast.
You can come any way you like.

But we would like you to come.
Christ invites you to come.
Please come.

CHARGE

The blessing and charge may be led from the doors of the church.

In the words of Paul,
"Beloved, whatever is true,
whatever is honorable,
whatever is just,
whatever is pure,
whatever is pleasing,
whatever is commendable,
if there is any excellence
and if there is anything worthy of praise,
think about these things."
Amen. *or* **Thanks be to God.**

Proper 24

October 16–22

SEMICONTINUOUS READINGS

Exodus 33:12–23   1 Thessalonians 1:1–10
Psalm 99   Matthew 22:15–22

OPENING SENTENCES

> You have found favor in my sight,
> says the Lord;
> I know you by name.
> **Show us your glory.**
>
> My presence will go with you,
> and I will give you rest.
> **Where you are is our rest!**

PRAYER OF THE DAY

> We come before you today, O God,
> to worship you in your holy splendor.
> Our hearts tremble before you,
> mindful of your goodness and mercy.
> Show us your glory, we pray.
> Reveal your presence with us
> that we may be strengthened and sustained,
> now and for the journey to come;
> in Jesus' name we pray. **Amen.**

INVITATION TO DISCIPLESHIP

The invitation to discipleship may be led from the baptismal font.

> Paul wrote to the church of the Thessalonians,
> "Grace to you and peace.
> We always give thanks to God for all of you
> and mention you in our prayers,
> constantly remembering before our God and Father
> your work of faith and labor of love
> and steadfastness of hope in our Lord Jesus Christ."

He called them to remember that God had chosen them
and that, through the Holy Spirit,
their work had made a difference.

As a community of faith,
we are called to support each other
as Paul supported the Thessalonians.
We strive to lift up and call out
the gifts we see in each other,
to encourage each other in our faith,
and to walk the journey of faith together.
If you are seeking to live out your faith
in a supportive community, please join us.

PRAYERS OF INTERCESSION

The prayers of intercession may be led from the midst of the congregation.

Lover of justice,
you are quick to answer the pleas of your people.
Hear our prayer:

For the church to reflect your glory . . .
that we may shine in the light of your truth
and dispel the lies that give shade to oppressors.

For the humbling of nations . . .
that they might know they are not above you, God,
and that they are not the judges of people's lives.

For our neighborhoods . . .
that they would not harbor segregation,
but be a place of welcome to all.

For freedom . . .
that those locked up by courts of injustice,
chained by predatory lending,
and imprisoned in their own self-hatred
may find liberation at last.

All this we pray through Jesus Christ,
the anointed servant of your justice. **Amen.**

INVITATION TO OFFERING

The invitation to offering may be led from the Communion table.

Look carefully at your hands
and everything that is in them.
Doesn't everything have a reflection
of the image of God?
Doesn't everything come from the earth,
which is the work of God?

Then let us give to God what comes from God.

INVITATION TO THE TABLE

The invitation to the table is led from the Communion table.

Moses asked God for a sign;
he asked to see God's glory.
At God's table
we are given a glimpse of God's glory
when the earthly elements of bread and cup
become a sign of God's heavenly feast.

This table has room for you and room for all.
Because God has been gracious to us,
because God has shown mercy to us,
we come to this table to rest, to be fed,
and to join with believers in every time and place.

Come, be fed, and know that you belong to God.

CHARGE

The blessing and charge may be led from the doors of the church.

When Moses was feeling anxious about the work before him,
he asked God for a sign; Moses wanted to see God's glory.
God passed by him, saying,
"You have found favor in my sight, and I know you by name. . . .
I will be gracious to whom I will be gracious,
and will show mercy on whom I will show mercy."
Look for God's glory this week,
aware that God's grace and mercy
may be resting on the people you least expect.
God knows you by name.
May God's presence go with you and give you rest.
Amen. *or* **Thanks be to God.**

Proper 24

October 16–22

COMPLEMENTARY READINGS

Isaiah 45:1–7
Psalm 96:1–9 (10–13)

1 Thessalonians 1:1–10
Matthew 22:15–22

OPENING SENTENCES

> O sing to the Lord a new song;
> sing to the Lord, all the earth.
> **Sing to the Lord, bless God's name;**
> **tell of God's salvation from day to day.**
>
> Declare God's glory among the nations,
> the Lord's marvelous works among all the peoples.
> **For great is the Lord**
> **and greatly to be praised.**

PRAYER OF THE DAY

> God of justice,
> who shatters prison doors
> and cuts iron bars,
> strengthen our hands
> so we may imitate Christ
> in leveling mountains
> and establishing equity.
> Spirit of Christ,
> flow through every cell
> like rich oxygen,
> that every breath
> might be joyous praise. **Amen.**

INVITATION TO DISCIPLESHIP

The invitation to discipleship may be led from the baptismal font.

God isn't one to let injustice persist.
God rescues the people from Pharaoh's grip.
So don't shy away from your calling.
You are the people of God—
breaking down doors that exclude,
dismantling walls that divide,
and loosening chains of addiction.

We are witnesses of God's glory,
so beautiful and strong.
The glory of God beams
from our whole body.
Our words and deeds
are shining with the will of God.

PRAYERS OF INTERCESSION

The prayers of intercession may be led from the midst of the congregation.

Great are you, Lord,
and greatly to be praised.

For the gift of this day, we are grateful.
With voices joined together,
singing your praise, in songs new and old,
reveal to us the gifts we can only find in community.
Working toward your vision of a peace that will last,
we seek your direction and guidance.
Great are you, Lord,
and greatly to be praised.

We offer prayers for those who are ill, in pain,
grieving, and carrying the weight of the world.
May we set down the burdens we carry,
the worries that fester,
and the concerns we carry for each other and ourselves.
You are the great healer.
Be gracious to us.
Show us your mercy.
Great are you, Lord,
and greatly to be praised.

Hear our prayers for the nations.
At our best, we are a pale approximation
of your realm of justice and mercy.
Too often we are not at our best.
We offer prayers for all in harm's way
because of governments that value power and wealth
over peace and wholeness.
Turn our hearts toward your glory,
that we may build societies
where care for each other trumps selfish gain.
May our work reflect your dreams.
May our hopes create your peace.
Great are you, Lord,
and greatly to be praised.

The trees should sing with joy,
and the earth should rejoice.
Help us care for your creation as you do.
May we heal the rivers so the seas will roar with life.
May we tend to the fields that they may be
healed and restored,
bringing forth abundance for all.
Great are you, Lord,
and greatly to be praised.

We offer these prayers with hope for the world.
Lead us to turn our hopes into actions,
that the world may see a glimpse of your glory. **Amen.**

INVITATION TO OFFERING

The invitation to offering may be led from the Communion table.

The psalmist proclaims,
"All the gods of the peoples are idols,
but the Lord made the heavens.
Honor and majesty are before the Lord;
strength and beauty are in God's sanctuary.
Ascribe to the Lord, O families of the peoples,
ascribe to the Lord glory and strength.
Ascribe to the Lord the glory due God's name;
bring an offering, and come into God's courts."

As our offering is received this day,
let us return to the Lord a portion of what we have received,
ascribing to the Lord the glory due God's name.

INVITATION TO THE TABLE

The invitation to the table is led from the Communion table.

This is the table of the Lord,
where everyone has a seat and is called by name.
Those excluded from the tables of the world
have a place at this table.

We are here by the gracious invitation of Jesus—
all of us, though sinners and undeserving.
We all belong to God, and to each other.

CHARGE

The blessing and charge may be led from the doors of the church.

The days of injustice are numbered.
God is on the move against the emperors of the world.
Their rebellion comes from fear.
So fear not!
Held by God's love and righteousness,
speak the truth wherever you go.
Amen. *or* **Thanks be to God.**

Proper 25

October 23–29

SEMICONTINUOUS READINGS

Deuteronomy 34:1–12   1 Thessalonians 2:1–8
Psalm 90:1–6, 13–17   Matthew 22:34–46

OPENING SENTENCES

Lord, you have been our dwelling place
in all generations.
**Before the mountains were brought forth
or ever you had formed the earth and the world,
from everlasting to everlasting you are God.**

PRAYER OF THE DAY

Lord, you are our dwelling place.
In you we find our rest.
Gather us in under the shelter of your wing.
Settle our souls and calm our minds,
that we may worship you this day
in joy and peace. **Amen.**

INVITATION TO DISCIPLESHIP

The invitation to discipleship may be led from the baptismal font.

When Jesus was asked,
"Teacher, which commandment in the law is the greatest?"
he had no trouble answering:
"'You shall love the Lord your God
with all your heart, and with all your soul,
and with all your mind.'
This is the greatest and first commandment.
And a second is like it:
'You shall love your neighbor as yourself.'
On these two commandments hang all the law
and the prophets."

If you'd like to help in answering the world's questions,
we try to be part of the answer.
I invite you to journey with us—
hearts, souls, and minds,
seeking to love and serve the Lord.

PRAYERS OF INTERCESSION

The prayers of intercession may be led from the midst of the congregation.

Lord, you have been our dwelling place
in all generations.
You brought forth the mountains.
You formed the earth and the world,
and from everlasting to everlasting you are God.
We are your grateful people,
thankful that you are mindful of us.
We are bold to come before you with our worries,
with our hopes, with our dreams,
knowing you hear the prayers of your faithful children.

For the gift of this day
and the chance to gather together,
we are thankful.
Draw us ever closer to you and to each other,
that we may feel our connectedness
and know how much we matter to you and to our neighbors.

We want to love you with our hearts, souls, and minds,
so keep us centered on your mercy,
that we may extend your love to our world.

We offer prayers this day for our neighbors far away,
in the path of extreme weather, extreme politics,
or other challenges that isolate and separate us from each other.

We offer prayers for our neighbors nearby—
the ones we know and like,
the ones we aren't sure we're so fond of,
the ones we haven't met yet,
and the ones who would deny we are neighbors at all.

Help us love each other as you love us,
that we may create a safer world for all your children.
From everlasting to everlasting, you are God. **Amen.**

INVITATION TO OFFERING

The invitation to offering may be led from the Communion table.

God never forgot us
even when we gave up on ourselves,
forgetting our life's calling.
God didn't spare anything
to bring us to the promised land.

So why be stingy with our gratitude?
There is nothing more natural
than to give generously
to the One who has rescued us
and has given us new life.

INVITATION TO THE TABLE

The invitation to the table is led from the Communion table.

The command to love our neighbor as ourselves
is woven throughout the story of Scripture.
It is at this table where we see most clearly
how God teaches us to love our neighbor.
God sets a table with room enough for all.
It is at this table where we are fed and nourished.
It is at this table where strangers become neighbors
and even become family.

Come to the table.

CHARGE

The blessing and charge may be led from the doors of the church.

> Moses died just shy of the promised land.
> Sometimes our journey of faith is like that.
> We get the wandering and the wilderness,
> but the end may be hard to see.
> We plant trees so others will harvest the fruit.
> We build structures and societies
> that will benefit generations down the road.
> Don't let the distance from the finish line
> keep you from enjoying the journey.
> Let us journey on,
> heading toward the promised land together.
> **Amen.** *or* **Thanks be to God.**

Proper 25

October 23–29

COMPLEMENTARY READINGS

Leviticus 19:1–2, 15–18
Psalm 1

1 Thessalonians 2:1–8
Matthew 22:34–46

OPENING SENTENCES

Love the Lord your God!
Yes, we will love the Lord
with all our heart, mind, and soul!

Love your neighbor!
Yes, we will love our neighbors
as we would love ourselves,
as we would love God.

PRAYER OF THE DAY

Loving God,
you never break your promise.
You remember what you said,
then accomplish it in good time.
You have loved us
through the human hands of Jesus
and taught us to love like Jesus.
Holy Spirit, dwell in our bodies,
that our hands might bring healing like Jesus,
that our hands might be lifted in worship
that pleases you. **Amen.**

INVITATION TO DISCIPLESHIP

The invitation to discipleship may be led from the baptismal font.

Don't hide with sinners,
but come out to the light of righteousness.
There's sun and water to nurture you,
so you can bear fruit, no matter the season.

Don't be hungry for praise from mortals,
but seek God's approval.
It will satisfy your soul,
and you will hunger no more.

What does God approve of?
Neighborly love.
Care and concern for the welfare
of those who are near us,
of those who are in need of God,
as we all are.

PRAYERS OF INTERCESSION

The prayers of intercession may be led from the midst of the congregation.

God, you lavish loving attention on us.
Remember us this day as we lift up our prayers:

We pray for your church . . .
Teach us to love you, God,
by loving this world,
for you sent us to love this world,
just as you sent your Son
because you loved this world.

We pray for this world you love . . .
There is pain and hurt in the land.
There is sin and hatred in the land.
Poisoned by human greed,
the land has grown toxic.
Renew this land and restore our hearts.

Hold us tenderly,
like a mother nursing her child.
Let us not be swept away
like husks of grain in the wind.
Meet us today, face to face.
Burn off our self-deceit.
We want to know you.
We want to be known by you;
through Jesus Christ our Lord. **Amen.**

INVITATION TO OFFERING

The invitation to offering may be led from the Communion table.

We are made holy because God is holy,
and we belong to God.
Our holiness doesn't make us better than other people.
It connects us to other people.
Because they also belong to God,
and God is holy, so they are holy.

We participate in the work of loving our neighbor as ourselves
with our tithes and our offerings.
We set apart a portion of what we have been given.
We declare it holy,
because God is holy,
and we belong to God.

As our offering is received this day,
let us give with joyful hearts, made holy by love.

INVITATION TO THE TABLE

The invitation to the table is led from the Communion table.

This is the Lord's table—
where the powerful and the weak,
the rich and the poor,
the addict and the A-student
sit together,
without judgment and without envy.
There is nothing to envy,
because we see ourselves as Christ sees us—
everyone both broken and sacred.

Don't count yourself out of this feast.
Enjoy this endless banquet of divine love.
**Jesus, we thank you
for welcoming us as guests of honor.**

CHARGE

The blessing and charge may be led from the doors of the church.

Don't skimp on the good news.
There's enough bad news to go around.
Share the good news at every chance.
Speak it, sing it, and do it!
Amen. *or* **Thanks be to God.**

Proper 26

October 30–November 5

SEMICONTINUOUS READINGS

Joshua 3:7–17
Psalm 107:1–7, 33–37

1 Thessalonians 2:9–13
Matthew 23:1–12

OPENING SENTENCES

Draw near and hear:
God's love endures forever.
**Your love sets us dancing
and worshiping you with great joy!**

PRAYER OF THE DAY

God,
when we got lost
in a wilderness of our own making,
you guided us safely to the waters of your love.
Jesus,
you offered yourself as water
to refresh us for the journey ahead.
Holy Spirit,
turn our gratitude into songs of praise,
in the holy worship of your name. **Amen.**

INVITATION TO DISCIPLESHIP

The invitation to discipleship may be led from the baptismal font.

God calls us to preach the Word.
But without faithfulness
our words ring hollow and turn people away.

So let your work lead your words.
Work for peace,
and resist violence.
Work for justice,
and don't participate in exploiting the excluded.
Jesus didn't just give teachings to repeat.
He became the life to imitate.

PRAYERS OF INTERCESSION

The prayers of intercession may be led from the midst of the congregation.

We give you thanks, O Lord, for you are good;
and your steadfast love endures forever.

We called to you and you rescued us from trouble,
gathering us from the east and from the west,
from the north and from the south.
We give you thanks, O Lord, for you are good,
and your steadfast love endures forever.

Thank you for your steadfast love,
for your wonderful works to humankind.
You satisfy the thirsty,
and the hungry you fill with good things.
May we be your agents of abundance
in a world of hungry and thirsty people.
We give you thanks, O Lord, for you are good,
and your steadfast love endures forever.

You turn a desert into pools of water,
a parched land into springs of water.
Rain down your mercy
into the dry and dusty corners of our lives.
Quench our souls,
and let your justice flow as a river
through our lives, our communities, our world.
We give you thanks, O Lord, for you are good,
and your steadfast love endures forever.

God of all goodness and steadfast love,
receive the prayers we offer,
and let your will be done in our world;
through Jesus Christ our Savior. **Amen.**

INVITATION TO OFFERING

The invitation to offering may be led from the Communion table.

We have been given grace and mercy.

Let us share what we have received,
so others may know of God's expansive love.

INVITATION TO THE TABLE

The invitation to the table is led from the Communion table.

We are at the Lord's table
because God has brought us
through storms and droughts,
through deep waters and hungry fires.
We've made it to God's home,
with nothing to boast about
except the story of our lifelong gratitude.

Come and taste the bread,
the bread of grace.
Come and taste the wine,
the wine of grace.

CHARGE

The blessing and charge may be led from the doors of the church.

Keep going forward
one step at a time.
Before every step,
God goes ahead
and clears the path.
Water or fire,
you will walk right through them all.
So keep going.
Amen. *or* **Thanks be to God.**

Proper 26

October 30–November 5

COMPLEMENTARY READINGS

Micah 3:5–12   1 Thessalonians 2:9–13
Psalm 43   Matthew 23:1–12

OPENING SENTENCES

O send out your light and your truth, O Lord.
Let them lead me to your holy hill
and to your dwelling place.

Then I will go to the altar of God,
to the God of my exceeding joy.
I will praise you with the harp, O God.

Why are you cast down, O my soul,
and why are you disquieted within me?
Hope in God,
for I shall again praise the Lord,
my help and my God.

PRAYER OF THE DAY

Lead us, O God,
by your light and your truth.
You are our hope and our refuge.
Focus our hearts on your word this day,
that we may worship you in joy and hope. **Amen.**

---

*The greatest among you will be your servant. All who
exalt themselves will be humbled, and all who humble
themselves will be exalted.*

Matthew 23:11–12

INVITATION TO DISCIPLESHIP

The invitation to discipleship may be led from the baptismal font.

Discipleship is a challenge
when the world can't agree
on which prophets are true and which are false.
Many different voices compete for your time,
your talents, your allegiance.

If you're looking for a group of people
who are seeking to discern God's truth
and God's hopes for the world,
please join us here.
We don't have all the answers,
but we value all your questions.

PRAYERS OF INTERCESSION

The prayers of intercession may be led from the midst of the congregation.

Jesus doesn't hold back
any good things from us,
so confidently we ask
for God's generous blessing in the world.
Hear our prayer, O God.

For the church in all nations . . .
that we would be people
who step into the rivers that divide people,
making a pathway to reconciliation.

For the leaders of nations . . .
that they would know
that your kin-dom demands
an account of the ways
they led and cared for their people.

For migrants and refugees . . .
that, though they might be without a nation,
they may know they are not without you, God,
and that they are citizens of your world,
with rights to fellowship with all your people.

For this earth and all its creatures . . .
that all may flourish,
from trees that mark the seasons
to birds that seek their way home.

For humanity . . .
that we may be more faithful as stewards,
leaving the earth better
than when it was entrusted to us.

Show us your blessing, O God,
and make us a blessing in your world;
through Jesus Christ our Savior. **Amen.**

INVITATION TO OFFERING

The invitation to offering may be led from the Communion table.

If we have a choice to decide
how much to give to the work of God,
it means we are more privileged than others.
How can one be a miser
when one has received such mercy?

Give freely,
give generously,
give joyously.

INVITATION TO THE TABLE

The invitation to the table is led from the Communion table.

At God's table there is room enough for all.
The prophets warned against religious leaders
who tried to lead God's people astray,
who tried to limit and control God's mercy and grace
for their own power and image.

If you've been excluded from God's table,
or God's welcome, or God's family
by people speaking in God's name, we apologize.
You deserved better.

Because God is love.
And God's welcome will be wide.
And God's table reaches into eternity.
All of who you are is welcome here.
Come, and be fed.

CHARGE

The blessing and charge may be led from the doors of the church.

As people who have been fed at God's table,
we go from this place to feed others.
Carry God's abundance into the world.
Let your actions of faith speak louder
than the false prophets of fear.
Amen. *or* **Thanks be to God.**

All Saints' Day

November 1 or first Sunday in November

Revelation 7:9–17　　　　1 John 3:1–3
Psalm 34:1–10, 22　　　　Matthew 5:1–12

OPENING SENTENCES

O magnify the Lord with me,
and let us exalt God's name together.
Salvation belongs to our God,
who is seated on the throne, and to the Lamb!

O taste and see that the Lord is good;
happiness comes to those
who take refuge in the Lord.
Salvation belongs to our God,
who is seated on the throne, and to the Lamb!

The Lord redeems the life of the faithful;
none who take refuge in God will see punishment.
Salvation belongs to our God,
who is seated on the throne, and to the Lamb!

O magnify the Lord with me,
and let us exalt God's name together.
Gathered in the presence of all the saints,
let us worship the God of our salvation.

PRAYER OF THE DAY

God of all,
Lamb of salvation and Shepherd of your people,
we long for the day when trials are ended,
when hunger and thirst will cease,
and when sorrow and suffering will be no more.
Until that day,
guide us by your Word and Spirit,
that we may find our place among the saints,
whose very lives proclaim your promise;
through Christ our Lord. **Amen.**

INVITATION TO DISCIPLESHIP

The invitation to discipleship may be led from the baptismal font.

See what love the Father has given us,
that we should be called children of God;
and that is what we are.

If you desire to know this love, then come.
Embraced by the imperfect communion
of the children of God,
you are invited into the divine fellowship
of God's saints in glory.

PRAYERS OF INTERCESSION

The prayers of intercession may be led from the midst of the congregation.

God of all, in your great love
you have called us children
and have promised to hear us when we cry to you.
Joining all the saints,
we lift our prayer before your throne.

God of peace, we remember before you
those who are tormented by anxiety or depression
and those whose lives are tormented by violence and war.
We remember the poor and the afflicted,
the sick and the dying,
prisoners and all who are lonely.
Help us, your children,
to be makers of peace.
Joining all the saints,
we lift our prayer before your throne.

God of righteousness, we remember before you
those who do not know the hope of your future
and those who do not know safety and refuge.
We remember those caught in cycles of poverty,
young ones who go uncared for,
lives threatened by prejudice and hate.
Help us, your children,
to hunger and thirst for righteousness.
Joining all the saints,
we lift our prayer before your throne.

God of mercy, we remember before you
those who seek your blessing
in a world that is broken and battered,
and those whose cries are silenced—
the cries of the faithful, silenced by persecution;
the cries of the merciful, silenced by injustice;
the cries of the hopeful, silenced by oppression.
Help us, your children,
to be agents of mercy.
Joining all the saints,
we lift our prayer before your throne.

God of eternity,
we thank you for all the saints—
those recognized broadly
and those whose quiet lives of faith
are known only to a few.
We rejoice that they have taken their place
in the company of heaven,
even as we remember them before you . . .

Names may be lifted silently or aloud.

Help us, your church, to be guided by their example
into humble service and bold faith
until we too have come out of the great ordeal
and are joined in eternal praise
before your throne. **Amen.**

INVITATION TO OFFERING

The invitation to offering may be led from the Communion table.

The psalmist assures us
that those who seek the Lord lack no good thing.

Having received from the Lord,
let us make an offering
to the one who offered himself for us,
joining in the labors of the saints
to the glory of God
and the blessing of God's servants.

INVITATION TO THE TABLE

The invitation to the table is led from the Communion table.

From earth's wide bounds,
from ocean's farthest coast,
our Savior gathers the multitudes
to sit at his table in glory.

For all who are thirsty, this is the place to receive living water.
For all who hunger, this is the place to be fed.
For all who sorrow, this is the place
where God will taste the salt of your tears.
For all who rejoice, this is the place
where God will rejoice over you with singing.

Come to this table with one another
and with all the saints who have gone before you.
Come, taste and see that the Lord is good.

CHARGE

The blessing and charge may be led from the doors of the church.

Saints of the living God,
rejoice and be glad.
For by the Father's love
you are called children of God,
and that is what you are.
Amen. *or* **Thanks be to God.**

Proper 27

November 6–12

SEMICONTINUOUS READINGS

Joshua 24:1–3a, 14–25   1 Thessalonians 4:13–18
Psalm 78:1–7   Matthew 25:1–13

OPENING SENTENCES

Give ear, O people, to my teachings.
Incline your ears to the words of my mouth.
We open our lips in parables;
we utter dark sayings from of old.

These are things we have heard and known,
that our ancestors have told us.
We will not hide them from our children;
we will tell the coming generation
the glorious deeds of the Lord.

PRAYER OF THE DAY

Your covenant is all we seek, O God.
Silence in us any voice but yours this day.
Help us sort through the clutter
and distractions in our lives,
that we may be present, here, right now,
and worship you in joy and peace. **Amen.**

---

*"Now if you are unwilling to serve the LORD, choose
this day whom you will serve, whether the gods your
ancestors served in the region beyond the River or the
gods of the Amorites in whose land you are living; but
as for me and my household, we will serve the LORD."*

Joshua 24:15

INVITATION TO DISCIPLESHIP

The invitation to discipleship may be led from the baptismal font.

When Joshua led the Israelites into the promised land,
he called on them to choose.
Choose this day whom you will serve.
God's grace is compelling.
It draws us to God.
But ultimately, it is our choice to follow God.

Are you ready to choose God,
maybe for the first time or maybe in a new way?
However you came to be here today,
we're glad you're here.
Whatever you choose,
you are always and already loved by God.
You are welcome here.

PRAYERS OF INTERCESSION

The prayers of intercession may be led from the midst of the congregation.

Holy Mystery, we seek you.
We want to choose you.
But your voice is drowned out
in the busyness of our lives.
Still our hearts.
Calm our minds.
Let us rest in your presence right now.

We offer prayers for this earth
on which we live out our lives.
You have given us Eden,
a garden of abundance and beauty.
We have not been careful stewards.
We have let our lamps go out,
and now we worry it might be too late.
But every act of conservation
is a choice toward a future with hope.
Lead us to care for your creation as you do.

Hear our prayers for our choices.
May they be thoughtful, deliberate, hopeful, and kind.
May our choices reflect our hopes for a better tomorrow.
May we always feel we have the agency to choose—
for our faith journeys,
for our life choices,
for our hopes and dreams.

We pray for those we know in need of your healing,
your peace, your comfort, and your courage.
Bring us to wholeness
and away from despair.
Lead us into supportive community
and away from isolation.
Guide us in our ministry,
that we may offer your healing to a hurting world.

In all these prayers we turn to you,
the author of our lives and the healer of the world. **Amen.**

INVITATION TO OFFERING

The invitation to offering may be led from the Communion table.

As the offering is received this day,
the choice is ours.

May our offerings reflect our hopes, not our fears.
May we choose abundance over scarcity.
May the story we tell of our lives
reflect the grace and mercy of God's provision
all along the way.

INVITATION TO THE TABLE

The invitation to the table is led from the Communion table.

Jesus often started his parables by saying,
"The kingdom of heaven will be like this . . ."
All of his stories pointed to God's realm,
where justice rolls down like waters
and righteousness like an ever-flowing stream.
The kingdom of heaven will be like this table,
where we are invited to a feast not of our own making,
where there is room for all,
where we are nourished and sustained.

Come to the table.
The kingdom of heaven is like this.

CHARGE

The blessing and charge may be led from the doors of the church.

Choose this day whom you will serve.
God's call on our life is joyful,
invitational, and life-giving.
And it is up to us to choose how to respond.
Go into the world,
remembering that your choices matter.
Amen. *or* **Thanks be to God.**

Proper 27

November 6–12

COMPLEMENTARY READINGS

Wisdom 6:12–16 *or*
   Amos 5:18–24
Wisdom 6:17–20 *or*
   Psalm 70

1 Thessalonians 4:13–18
Matthew 25:1–13

OPENING SENTENCES

Wisdom is radiant and unfading.
**She is easily discerned by those who love her
and is found by those who seek her.**

She hastens to make herself known
to those who desire her.
**One who rises early to seek her
will have no difficulty,
for she will be found sitting at the gate.**

PRAYER OF THE DAY

God,
you do not care for our worship
if we do not care for your justice.
Jesus,
you overturned tables in the temple,
angry at how we turned your house of prayer
into a marketplace.
Holy Spirit,
lead us in daily repentance,
that our service this day
may be a delight to you
as we worship in spirit and in truth. **Amen.**

INVITATION TO DISCIPLESHIP

The invitation to discipleship may be led from the baptismal font.

If you are not prepared,
the day of the Lord
will be confusion, not light.

Discipleship is about making habits
that help us to become people
who welcome the Lord's return.
Discipleship is about becoming
people who know how to play the drums of justice,
who cultivate flowers of forgiveness,
who know how to stand up for truth
even when our knees buckle.

PRAYERS OF INTERCESSION

The prayers of intercession may be led from the midst of the congregation.

We are people of resurrection.
We grieve, but we grieve with hope.
We pray because we have hope
even in silence and shades of despair.
In Christ's life-giving power we pray.

We lift up the church . . .
Help us to bring you delight
in the daily walk of doing justice.
Let us never forget that you care more
about how we live for you
than what we say about you,
about what we do between our gatherings
than what we say when we gather.

We lift up the families of the earth . . .
Bring those who are in bondage
through debt or depression
out into the joy of freedom.
Be the presence of hope
for those who are grieving loved ones
by grieving with them.

In all our prayers, we are simply asking
that you do what you have promised
and what you have accomplished through the ages:
to rescue the poor, the needy, and the broken.
In Jesus' name we pray. **Amen.**

INVITATION TO OFFERING

The invitation to offering may be led from the Communion table.

We come to offer reverence
through a life of sincerity and faithfulness.
We come to offer our services
through our giving.

Let us be God's light of hope
through the offering of our lives.
Let us venture into places void of joy
to bring God's blessing to all.

INVITATION TO THE TABLE

The invitation to the table is led from the Communion table.

To come to the table of the Lord
requires no qualification of wealth or status,
not even righteousness.
But we cannot come with other gods
filling our stomach.
We must come empty,
empty and hungry for substantial food
that will nourish us, body and soul.
And we cannot come with pride,
because the proud are too arrogant
to accept the invitation,
or to sit with people
who are broken as they are.

So, hungry and humble,
let us come to the table.

CHARGE

The blessing and charge may be led from the doors of the church.

As people rescued by God,
you are God's salvation song.
Sing the joy of salvation
to those who are alone
and desperate for human connection.
Sing the joy of salvation
to those who are forgotten in prison,
and work until you can get them out.
Sing the joy of salvation
even to those who are imprisoned in arrogance
and believe they don't need rescuing.
As people rescued by God,
you are God's salvation song.
Amen. *or* **Thanks be to God.**

Proper 28

SEMICONTINUOUS READINGS

Judges 4:1–7　　　　　　　　1 Thessalonians 5:1–11
Psalm 123　　　　　　　　　　Matthew 25:14–30

OPENING SENTENCES

> To you I lift up my eyes, O God,
> enthroned in the heavens.
> **Our eyes look to you, O Lord;**
> **have mercy on us.**
>
> Have mercy on us, O Lord,
> for we have had too much contempt.
> **Our eyes look to you, O Lord;**
> **have mercy on us.**

PRAYER OF THE DAY

> Lord God, throughout our history
> you have raised up faithful leaders
> to deliver us from oppression,
> like the prophet Deborah.
> Heed the cries of those
> who are suffering in the world today
> and deliver them by your mighty hand,
> that they may know and trust
> the promise of your steadfast love;
> through Jesus Christ our Savior. **Amen.**

For God has destined us not for wrath but for obtaining salvation through our Lord Jesus Christ, who died for us, so that whether we are awake or asleep we may live with him.

1 Thessalonians 5:9–10

INVITATION TO DISCIPLESHIP

The invitation to discipleship may be led from the baptismal font.

As disciples of Jesus, we are called
to encourage one another
and build each other up
as we await the coming of Christ in glory.

How can we encourage you
in your journey of discipleship?
How can we help to build you up
in the practice of your faith?

PRAYERS OF INTERCESSION

The prayers of intercession may be led from the midst of the congregation.

O Lord our God,
in our distress we cry out for help.
Deliver us from evil.

From violence and destruction . . .
O Lord our God, **deliver us.**

From oppression and exploitation . . .
O Lord our God, **deliver us.**

From cruelty and contempt . . .
O Lord our God, **deliver us.**

From abuse and excess . . .
O Lord our God, **deliver us.**

From faithlessness and fear . . .
O Lord our God, **deliver us.**

From illness and affliction . . .
O Lord our God, **deliver us.**

From our own sorrow and sin . . .
O Lord our God, **deliver us.**

Deliver us from evil, O Lord our God,
for the kingdom, the power,
and the glory are yours,
now and forever. **Amen.**

INVITATION TO OFFERING

The invitation to offering may be led from the Communion table.

While we await Christ's coming,
God calls us to be good stewards
of the gifts of earth, of our lives,
and of this community of faith.

What have you done with the gifts
God has entrusted to your care?
How will you share what you have
in the service of Christ's realm?

INVITATION TO THE TABLE

The invitation to the table is led from the Communion table.

You know what time it is.
This is the day of our salvation.
This is the feast of our redemption.

Come, children of God.
The table of the Lord has been prepared.
Let us prepare our hearts to meet Christ here.

CHARGE

The blessing and charge may be led from the doors of the church.

Put on the breastplate of faith and love
and, for a helmet, the hope of salvation.
God has destined us not for wrath
but for salvation through our Lord Jesus Christ.
Amen. *or* **Thanks be to God.**

Proper 28

November 13–19

COMPLEMENTARY READINGS

Zephaniah 1:7, 12–18

Psalm 90:1–8 (9–11), 12

1 Thessalonians 5:1–11

Matthew 25:14–30

OPENING SENTENCES

> Lord, you have been our dwelling place
> in all generations.
> **From everlasting to everlasting
> you are God.**
>
> A thousand years in your sight
> are like yesterday.
> **You sweep them away
> like a dream.**
>
> All our days pass away;
> our years come to an end like a sigh.
> **Teach us to count our days,
> that we may have wise hearts.**

PRAYER OF THE DAY

> Holy One, you give us gifts
> for the service of your eternal realm
> and call us to use them wisely.
> Teach us not to hide our talents
> but to multiply them by your grace,
> that all may know the abundance
> of the new creation that is coming;
> through Jesus Christ our Lord. **Amen.**

INVITATION TO DISCIPLESHIP

The invitation to discipleship may be led from the baptismal font.

Jesus says the reign of God
is like a person who goes on a journey,
entrusting their property
to servants who remain at home.

How will you use the gifts of God
for the service of others?
How will you prepare yourself—
and this world that God loves—
for the return of Christ in glory?

PRAYERS OF INTERCESSION

The prayers of intercession may be led from the midst of the congregation.

As children of a new creation
we are called to pray without ceasing
while we await the day of the Lord.

Lord, hear our prayers:

For the wisdom to understand
the times and seasons . . .

For the strength to keep watch
through the hours of the night . . .

For true peace and security
and deliverance from destruction . . .

For the well-being of our bodies
and the sobriety of our spirits . . .

For the gifts of faith, love,
and the hope of salvation . . .

God of peace, make us holy.
Keep us safe in body and soul
until the coming of our Lord Jesus Christ,
in whose name we pray. **Amen.**

INVITATION TO OFFERING

The invitation to offering may be led from the Communion table.

> The Lord has been our dwelling place
> throughout the generations.
> Here, in the house of the Lord,
> we offer the gifts of our lives
> to the One who has given us life.
>
> Let us present our offerings to the Lord.

INVITATION TO THE TABLE

The invitation to the table is led from the Communion table.

> The day of the Lord is at hand!
> God has prepared a banquet for us
> and has consecrated the guests.
> God has gone out searching for us
> and now calls us to the table.
>
> Come in awe and wonder.
> Come with thanksgiving and joy.
> The feast of salvation is prepared for us.

CHARGE

The blessing and charge may be led from the doors of the church.

> The day of the Lord is at hand!
> Keep awake, then,
> for we belong to the day.
> **Amen.** *or* **Thanks be to God.**

Christ the King/Reign of Christ

November 20–26

SEMICONTINUOUS READINGS

Ezekiel 34:11–16, 20–24
Psalm 100

Ephesians 1:15–23
Matthew 25:31–46

OPENING SENTENCES

Make a joyful noise to the Lord, all the earth.
Worship the Lord with gladness;
come into God's presence with singing.

Know that the Lord is God.
The Lord made us,
and we belong to our Creator;
we are God's people
and the sheep of God's pasture.

Enter God's gates with thanksgiving
and the courts of the Lord with praise.
Give thanks to God; bless God's name.

For the Lord is good;
God's steadfast love endures forever
and God's faithfulness to all generations.

PRAYER OF THE DAY

Sovereign God,
in your steadfast love and faithfulness
you relentlessly seek us
and gather us into your presence.
Help us likewise to seek you,
for you have told us where you may be found—
not only in places of power and might
but in every place where your people cry out in need.
As we meet you in this service of worship,
send us out to meet you in acts of service,
doing justice and sharing your love;
through Christ our reigning Lord. **Amen.**

INVITATION TO DISCIPLESHIP

The invitation to discipleship may be led from the baptismal font.

Like lone sheep
we are prone to wander
in search of healing, meaning, belonging.
Like a good shepherd
Christ longs to bind up the injured,
to strengthen the weak,
and to bring back those who stray.

The One who gathers us here today
invites you to find all you are searching for
in the presence of our Shepherd and Savior.

PRAYERS OF INTERCESSION

The prayers of intercession may be led from the midst of the congregation.

Loving God, receive our prayers
with the tender presence of a shepherd
and the enduring power of a king.

Your Son,
once tempted in the wilderness,
hungry and alone,
reigns in glory now.
Gather into your presence
those who lack good food,
those who are malnourished and poor.
Empower us, your church,
to fill the hungry with good things.

Your Son,
once suspended on the cross,
crying out in thirst,
reigns in glory now.
Gather in your presence
those who long for clean water
in parched places and polluted waterways.
Empower us, your church,
to give drink to the thirsty.

Your Son,
once a stranger in Egypt,
seeking refuge,
reigns in glory now.
Gather in your presence
those in search of welcome—
the shelterless and the friendless.
Empower us, your church,
to welcome and support them.

Your Son,
once an infant in the manger,
naked and vulnerable,
reigns in glory now.
Gather in your presence
those in need of cover—
the cold, the exposed, the shamed.
Empower us, your church, to cover and encourage.

Your Son,
once praying in the garden,
sick with agony,
reigns in glory now.
Gather in your presence
those who are sick
in body, mind, or spirit.
Empower us, your church,
to offer healing and hope.

Your Son,
once judged and condemned,
a prisoner of injustice,
reigns in glory now.
Gather in your presence
those in prisons constructed by bars or fears,
by aging flesh or scattered minds.
Empower us, your church,
to speak release to the captives.

Loving God,
by your presence and your power
make your glorious reign known
even now. **Amen.**

INVITATION TO OFFERING

The invitation to offering may be led from the Communion table.

Come, you who are blessed by God.

Let us offer our gifts in service of Christ's kingdom,
that God's steadfast love might extend to all peoples
and God's faithfulness to all generations.

INVITATION TO THE TABLE

The invitation to the table is led from the Communion table.

The Good Shepherd gathers us
from all the places to which we have been scattered
to join in his kingdom feast.
It is not a feast reserved for the elite,
confined to halls of power and privilege,
gained by wealth or weapons.
It is a feast of abundance for all,
extended to every place where grace is needed,
received in humility and faith.

The Shepherd of your soul and King of all
welcomes you here.

CHARGE

The blessing and charge may be led from the doors of the church.

As God our Shepherd has searched for you,
search for Christ where he may be found,
empowered there to serve with love and justice.
Amen. *or* **Thanks be to God.**

Christ the King/Reign of Christ

November 20–26

COMPLEMENTARY READINGS

Ezekiel 34:11–16, 20–24   Ephesians 1:15–23
Psalm 95:1–7a   Matthew 25:31–46

OPENING SENTENCES

> O come, let us sing to the Lord;
> let us make a joyful noise to the rock of our salvation!
> Let us come into God's presence with thanksgiving;
> let us make a joyful noise with songs of praise!
> For the Lord is a great God
> and a great King above all gods.
>
> God's mighty hand
> holds earth's depths and mountain heights.
> God's compassionate hand
> formed the sea and the dry land.
> **O come, let us worship and bow down;**
> **let us kneel before the Lord, our Maker!**
>
> For the Lord is our God,
> **and we are the people of God's pasture**
> **and the sheep of God's hand.**

PRAYER OF THE DAY

> Almighty and everlasting God,
> King of all creation,
> we rejoice that your Son has triumphed over all powers
> and governs the nations with justice and righteousness.
> We give thanks that Christ is seated at your right hand
> and is head over all things for the sake of your church.
> By your Spirit, claim our complete loyalty
> and establish Christ's rule in every land and every heart.
> We pray in the name of Christ, who lives and reigns with you
> and the Holy Spirit, one God forever and ever. **Amen.**

INVITATION TO DISCIPLESHIP

The invitation to discipleship may be led from the baptismal font.

The One who holds the depths of the earth
and the heights of the mountains
holds you in strong hands
and wraps you in compassionate arms.
The One who reigns
above all power and dominion
longs to reign in your heart
and in your life.

Join us, as together we discover
the hope to which this One is calling us.

PRAYERS OF INTERCESSION

The prayers of intercession may be led from the midst of the congregation.

King of eternity,
our Savior and Judge,
in faith and love, we pray to you
as we watch for your coming in glory.

We remember in our prayers
the earth you have formed . . .
that pastures may be plentiful
and watercourses pure,
that the earth and all its creatures
may no longer be ravaged by greed or carelessness.
In faith and love, we pray to you
as we watch for your coming in glory.

We remember in our prayers
the nations of the world . . .
that the peoples may know peace and security
and communities may reflect your love,
that the actions and decisions of leaders
may be guided by your gracious sovereignty.
In faith and love, we pray to you
as we watch for your coming in glory.

We remember in our prayers
Christ's body, the church . . .
that we may proclaim your justice
and welcome those who have been cast aside,
that the hope to which you call us
may direct all our living.
In faith and love, we pray to you
as we watch for your coming in glory.

We remember in our prayers
those you have given us to love . . .
that they may know your healing in injury or illness
and your power in suffering and weakness,
that those who feel scattered and lost
may find rest and refuge in you.
In faith and love, we pray to you
as we watch for your coming in glory.

In faith and love, we pray in the name of Christ,
who gathers the nations at his coming in glory. **Amen.**

INVITATION TO OFFERING

The invitation to offering may be led from the Communion table.

With gratitude for the glorious inheritance
we share in Christ Jesus our Lord,
let us offer our time, talent, and treasure,
that our risen and reigning Lord might be made known
through the immeasurable greatness of God's power
at work through our gifts and in our lives.

INVITATION TO THE TABLE

The invitation to the table is led from the Communion table.

> From the right hand of God in the heavenly places,
> Christ comes to share this meal with us,
> placing into our hands
> the bread of life and the cup of salvation,
> making us to be for the world his body,
> the fullness of him who fills all in all.
>
> So come, open your hands,
> that Christ may reign in your heart.

CHARGE

The blessing and charge may be led from the doors of the church.

> Go from this place
> in a spirit of wisdom and revelation,
> so that with the eyes of your heart enlightened,
> you may know that even now,
> Christ Jesus reigns in glory.
> **Amen.** *or* **Thanks be to God.**

Supplements for the
Narrative Lectionary

Genesis 39:1–23

Narrative Lectionary Year 1, 3
(with Matthew 5:11–12)

OPENING SENTENCES

Blessed are you when people revile you
and persecute you
and utter all kinds of evil against you falsely
on my account.
Rejoice and be glad,
for your reward is great in heaven,
for in the same way they persecuted the prophets
who were before you.

PRAYER OF THE DAY

O Lord our God, we give you thanks
that your steadfast love is with us,
even in times of danger and distress.
Keep us faithful in your service,
and prosper the work of our hands,
that all people may know and trust
your providence and protection;
through Jesus Christ our Savior. **Amen.**

INVITATION TO DISCIPLESHIP

The invitation to discipleship may be led from the baptismal font.

Like our ancestors in the faith
we face struggles and challenges.
Yet we seek to be faithful,
finding favor in the sight of the Lord.

The path of discipleship is never easy,
but we know that God is with us.
Will you join us in this calling?

PRAYERS OF INTERCESSION

The prayers of intercession may be led from the midst of the congregation.

Here in your house, O God,
we open our hearts before you,
trusting that you alone
can deliver us from our distress.
Receive our prayers.

We pray for those, like Joseph,
who are exploited through human trafficking.
Help them find their freedom,
and lead us to abolish these practices.

We pray for those, like Joseph,
who face temptation.
Strengthen them to turn from evil
and turn toward your way.

We pray for those, like Joseph,
who are falsely accused.
Restore their reputations,
and give them honor and dignity.

We pray for those, like Joseph,
who are targeted because of their race.
Put an end to prejudice and discrimination,
and grant justice to all peoples.

We pray for those, like Joseph,
who are wrongfully imprisoned.
Help them plead their case
and find release.

Protect your people, O God,
through your steadfast love.
Be near to us in our distress,
and show us your grace and favor.
Cover us with the righteousness of Christ,
in whose holy name we pray. **Amen.**

INVITATION TO OFFERING

The invitation to offering may be led from the Communion table.

Like Joseph, our ancestor in faith,
we are called to be good stewards
of the gifts entrusted to us by the Lord.

With gladness and generosity
let us offer our gifts to God,
from whom all blessings flow.

INVITATION TO THE TABLE

The invitation to the table is led from the Communion table.

Our Savior Jesus Christ
has welcomed us into the house of the Lord
and called us to share God's table.

In faith and faithfulness
let us share this holy feast.

CHARGE

The blessing and charge may be led from the doors of the church.

Be faithful in Christ's service,
and the Lord will bless your work.
Amen. *or* **Thanks be to God.**

Scripture Index

This is an index to the lectionary readings supported in this volume. Revised Common Lectionary readings are listed in regular type; supplemental readings for the Narrative Lectionary are listed in italics.

OLD TESTAMENT

Genesis

1:1–2:4a	30
6:9–22; 7:24; 8:14–19	38
12:1–9	44
18:1–15 (21:1–7)	50
21:8–21	56
22:1–14	63
24:34–38, 42–49, 58–67	69
25:19–34	76
28:10–19a	82
29:15–28	89
32:22–31	97
37:1–4, 12–28	103
39:1–23	*225*
45:1–15	110
50:15–21	142

Exodus

1:8–2:10	118
3:1–15	125
12:1–14	132
14:19–31	139
15:1b–11, 20–21	139
16:2–15	146
17:1–7	153
19:2–8a	53
20:1–4, 7–9, 12–20	160
32:1–14	167
33:12–23	174

Leviticus

19:1–2, 15–18	186

Deuteronomy

11:18–21, 26–28	41
34:1–12	182

Joshua

3:7–17	190
24:1–3a, 14–25	201

Judges

4:1–7	209

1 Kings

3:5–12	93
19:9–18	106

Psalms

1	186
8	30
13	63
17:1–7, 15	97
19	160
23	170
25:1–9	156
26:1–8	128
31:1–5, 19–24	41
33:1–12	44
34:1–10, 22	197

NEW TESTAMENT

Comprehensive Scripture Index for Year A

This is an index to the lectionary readings supported in volumes 1 and 2 for Year A. Revised Common Lectionary readings are listed in regular type; supplemental readings for the Narrative Lectionary are listed in italics.

OLD TESTAMENT

Genesis

1:1–2:4a	147 (A1), 30 (A2)
2:15–17; 3:1–7	119 (A1)
6:9–22; 7:24; 8:14–19	38 (A2)
7:1–5, 11–18; 8:6–18; 9:8–13	147 (A1)
12:1–4a	122 (A1)
12:1–9	44 (A2)
18:1–15 (21:1–7)	50 (A2)
21:8–21	56 (A2)
22:1–14	63 (A2)
22:1–18	147 (A1)
24:34–38, 42–49, 58–67	69 (A2)
25:19–34	76 (A2)
28:10–19a	82 (A2)
29:15–28	89 (A2)
32:22–31	97 (A2)
37:1–4, 12–28	103 (A2)
39:1–23	*225 (A2)*
45:1–15	110 (A2)
50:15–21	142 (A2)

Exodus

1:8–2:10	118 (A2)
3:1–15	125 (A2)
12:1–4 (5–10), 11–14	139 (A1)
12:1–14	132 (A2)
14:10–31; 15:20–21	147 (A1)
14:19–31	139 (A2)
15:1b–11, 20–21	139 (A2)
15:1b–13, 17–18	147 (A1)
16:2–15	146 (A2)
17:1–7	125 (A1), 153 (A2)
19:2–8a	53 (A2)
20:1–4, 7–9, 12–20	160 (A2)
24:12–18	102 (A1)
32:1–14	167 (A2)
33:12–23	174 (A2)

Leviticus

19:1–2, 9–18	90 (A1)
19:1–2, 15–18	186 (A2)

Numbers

11:24–30	192 (A1)

Deuteronomy

11:18–21, 26–28	98 (A1), 41 (A2)
30:15–20	87 (A1)
32:1–4, 7, 36a, 43a	147 (A1)
34:1–12	182 (A2)

Joshua

3:7–17	190 (A2)
24:1–3a, 14–25	201 (A2)

Judges

4:1–7	209 (A2)

1 Samuel

16:1–13	128 (A1)

1 Kings

3:5–12	93 (A2)
19:9–18	106 (A2)

Psalms

1	186 (A2)
2	102 (A1)
8	30 (A2)
13	63 (A2)
15	81 (A1)
16	147, 168 (A1)
17:1–7, 15	97 (A2)
19	147 (A1), 160 (A2)
22	142 (A1)
23	128, 175 (A1), 170 (A2)
25:1–9	156 (A2)
26:1–8	128 (A2)
27:1, 4–9	78 (A1)
29	72 (A1)
31:1–5, 15–16	178 (A1)
31:1–5, 19–24	98 (A1), 41 (A2)
31:9–16	134 (A1)
32	119 (A1)
33:1–12	44 (A2)
34:1–10, 22	197 (A2)
40:1–11	75 (A1)
42 and 43	147 (A1)
43	193 (A2)
45:10–17	69 (A2)
46	147 (A1), 38 (A2)
47	185 (A1)
50:7–15	47 (A2)
51:1–3	*200 (A1)*
51:1–17	116 (A1)
65:(1–8) 9–13	79 (A2)
66:8–20	182 (A1)
67	113 (A2)
68:1–10, 32–35	188 (A1)
69:7–10 (11–15), 16–18	59 (A2)
70	205 (A2)
72:1–7, 10–14	59 (A1)
72:1–7, 18–19	22 (A1)
78:1–4, 12–16	153 (A2)
78:1–7	201 (A2)
80:1–7, 17–19	30 (A1)
80:7–15	163 (A2)
85:8–13	106 (A2)
86:1–10, 16–17	56 (A2)
86:11–17	86 (A2)
89:1–4, 15–18	66 (A2)
90:1–6, 13–17	182 (A2)
90:1–8 (9–11), 12	212 (A2)
93	185 (A1)
95	125 (A1)
95:1–7a	219 (A2)
96	44 (A1)
96:1–9 (10–13)	178 (A2)
97	47 (A1)
98	50, 147 (A1)
99	102 (A1), 174 (A2)
100	53, 215 (A2)
103:(1–7) 8–13	142 (A2)
104:24–34, 35b	192 (A1)
105:1–6, 16–22, 45b	103 (A2)
105:1–6, 23–26, 45b	125 (A2)
105:1–6, 37–45	146 (A2)
105:1–11, 45b	89 (A2)
106:1–6, 19–23	167 (A2)
107:1–7, 33–37	190 (A2)
112:1–9 (10)	84 (A1)
114	147, 164 (A1), 139 (A2)
116:1–2, 12–19	139 (A1), 50 (A2)
116:1–4, 12–19	172 (A1)
118:1–2, 14–24	160 (A1)
118:1–2, 19–29	134 (A1)
119:1–8	87 (A1)
119:33–40	90 (A1), 135 (A2)
119:105–112	76 (A2)
119:129–136	93 (A2)
121	122 (A1)
122	18 (A1)
123	209 (A2)
124	118 (A2)
128	89 (A2)
130	131 (A1)
131	94 (A1), 34 (A2)
132:11–12	*197 (A1)*

John (*continued*)

14:1–14	178 (A1)
14:15–21	182 (A1)
17:1–11	188 (A1)
18:1–19:42	142 (A1)
20:1–18	147, 160 (A1)
20:19–23	192 (A1)
20:19–31	168 (A1)

Acts

1:1–11	185 (A1)
1:6–14	188 (A1)
2:1–21	192 (A1)
2:14a, 22–32	168 (A1)
2:14a, 36–41	172 (A1)
2:42–47	175 (A1)
7:55–60	178 (A1)
10:34–43	72, 160 (A1)
17:22–31	182 (A1)

Romans

1:1–7	30 (A1)
1:16–17; 3:22b–28 (29–31)	98 (A1), 38, 41 (A2)
4:1–5, 13–17	122 (A1)
4:13–25	44, 47 (A2)
5:1–8	50, 53 (A2)
5:1–11	125 (A1)
5:12–19	119 (A1)
6:1b–11	56, 59 (A2)
6:3–11	147 (A1)
6:12–23	63, 66 (A2)
7:15–25a	69, 73 (A2)
8:1–11	76, 79 (A2)
8:6–11	131 (A1)
8:12–25	82, 86 (A2)
8:26–39	89, 93 (A2)
9:1–5	97, 100 (A2)
10:5–15	103, 106 (A2)
11:1–2a, 29–32	110, 113 (A2)
12:1–8	118, 121 (A2)
12:9–21	125, 128 (A2)
13:8–14	132, 135 (A2)
13:11–14	18 (A1)
14:1–12	139, 142 (A2)
15:4–13	22 (A1)

1 Corinthians

1:1–9	75 (A1)
1:10–18	78 (A1)
1:18–31	81 (A1)
2:1–12 (13–16)	84 (A1)
3:1–9	87 (A1)
3:10–11, 16–23	90 (A1)
4:1–5	94 (A1), 34 (A2)
5:6b–8	164 (A1)
11:23–26	139 (A1)
12:3b–13	192 (A1)

2 Corinthians

5:20b–6:10	116 (A1)
13:11–13	30 (A2)

Ephesians

1:3–14	56 (A1)
1:15–23	185 (A1), 215, 219 (A2)
3:1–12	59 (A1)
5:8–14	128 (A1)

Philippians

1:21–30	146, 149 (A2)
2:1–13	153, 156 (A2)
2:5–11	134 (A1)
3:4b–14	160, 163 (A2)
4:1–9	167, 170 (A2)

Colossians

3:1–4	160 (A1)

1 Thessalonians

1:1–10	174, 178 (A2)
2:1–8	182, 186 (A2)
2:9–13	190, 193 (A2)
4:13–18	201, 205 (A2)
5:1–11	209, 212 (A2)

Titus

2:11–14	44 (A1)
3:4–7	47 (A1)

Hebrews

1:1–4 (5–12)	50 (A1)
2:10–18	53 (A1)
4:14–16; 5:7–9	142 (A1)
10:16–25	142 (A1)

Contributors

CLAUDIA L. AGUILAR RUBALCAVA, Pastor, First Mennonite Church, Denver

MAMIE BROADHURST, Co-Pastor, University Presbyterian Church, Baton Rouge, Louisiana

DAVID GAMBRELL, Associate for Worship, Office of Theology and Worship, Presbyterian Mission Agency, Presbyterian Church (U.S.A.), Louisville, Kentucky

MARCI AULD GLASS, Pastor and Head of Staff, Calvary Presbyterian Church, San Francisco

MARCUS A. HONG, Director of Field Education and Assistant Professor of Practical Theology, Louisville Presbyterian Theological Seminary, Louisville, Kentucky

KIMBERLY BRACKEN LONG, Liturgical Scholar, Cambridge, Maryland

EMILY MCGINLEY, Senior Pastor, City Church, San Francisco

KENDRA L. BUCKWALTER SMITH, Director of the Worship Program, Pittsburgh Theological Seminary, and Associate Pastor for Discipleship, Shadyside Presbyterian Church, Pittsburgh, Pennsylvania

SAMUEL SON, Manager of Diversity and Reconciliation, Executive Director's Office, Presbyterian Mission Agency, Presbyterian Church (U.S.A.), Louisville, Kentucky

SLATS TOOLE, Freelance Writer, Minneapolis

BYRON A. WADE, General Presbyter, Presbytery of Western North Carolina, Morganton, North Carolina